Presented To:

Presented By:

Date:

POWER OF PRONOUNCING BLESSING

Georgina Boye

WESTBOW
PRESS®
A DIVISION OF THOMAS NELSON
& ZONDERVAN

Scripture taken from the King James Version of the Bible.

WestBow Press books may be ordered through booksellers or by contacting:

WestBow Press
A Division of Thomas Nelson & Zondervan
1663 Liberty Drive
Bloomington, IN 47403
www.westbowpress.com
1 (866) 928-1240

ISBN: 978-1-4908-6373-3 (sc)
ISBN: 978-1-4908-6374-0 (hc)
ISBN: 978-1-4908-6372-6 (e)

Library of Congress Control Number: 2014922327

Print information available on the last page.

WestBow Press rev. date: 07/30/2015

This book is dedicated to my Creator and Father, Jesus Christ, My Lord and Savior and affectionately dedicated to The Holy Spirit, my senior Partner.

CONTENTS

Preface xi

Introduction xix

Chapter 1:   Pronouncing the Blessings of the Bible .. 1

Chapter 2:   Blessings for Financial Breakthrough ...49

Chapter 3:   Blessings on Your Body 53

Chapter 4:   Blessings on Your Clothing 57

Chapter 5:   Blessings on Your Business 61

Chapter 6:   Blessings on Your Place of Work 65

Chapter 7:   Blessings on Your Sons 69

Chapter 8:   Blessings on Your Daughters 73

Chapter 9:   Blessings on Your Young Children
              (Babies, Toddlers, Teens) 77

Chapter 10: Blessings on Your Land 83

Chapter 11: Blessings on Your Family (By the
              Father) 87

Chapter 12: Blessings on Your family (By the Mother) 89

Chapter 13: Blessings for Your Grandson 93

Chapter 14: Blessings on Your Granddaughter 95

Chapter 15: Blessings on Your Brother 97

Chapter 16: Blessings on Your Sister.................... 99

Chapter 17: Blessings on Your Uncle....................101

Chapter 18: Blessings on Your Aunt 103

Chapter 19: Blessings on Your Nephew.................105

Chapter 20: Blessings on Your Niece 107

Chapter 21: Blessings on Your Children's School...109

Chapter 22: Blessings on Your Children's Teachers 111

Chapter 23: Blessings on Your Male Child's Friends.................113

Chapter 24: Blessings on Your Female Child's Friends.................117

Chapter 25: Blessings on Your Wife's Friends 119

Chapter 26: Blessings on Your Husband's Friends .121

Chapter 27: Blessings on Your Neighbor 123

Chapter 28: Blessings on Your Boss......................125

Chapter 29: Blessings on Your Associates and Coworkers 129

Chapter 30: Blessings on Your Friends..................131

Chapter 31: Blessings on Your Family Friends.......133

Chapter 32: Blessings on Your Enemies..............135

Chapter 33: Blessings on Your Environment..........139

Chapter 34: Blessings for the Enlargement of
Your Coast.....................141

Chapter 35: Blessings on Local Businesses.............143

Chapter 36: Blessings on Your Land, Property,
or Estate......................147

Chapter 37: Blessings on Your Church.................151

Chapter 38: Blessings on Your Pastor...................157

Chapter 39: Blessings on Your Church Members...163

Chapter 40: Blessings on Christians and the
Church of the Lord Jesus Christ........165

Chapter 41: Blessings on Your Pets......................167

Chapter 42: Blessings on Your Food....................169

Chapter 43: Blessings on Your City or Village.......171

Chapter 44: Blessings on Your Country................173

Chapter 45: Blessings on Leaders of Your Nation..177

Chapter 46: Blessings of Law Enforcement Agents 181

Chapter 47: Blessings on Your Continent.............183

PREFACE

Blessings are very important in every living person's life. They must be pronounced on or conferred upon one.

This book will equip you to make the right pronouncements of blessing upon your loved ones. They are direct and to the point. Pronounce the blessings on what and who you love and wish the best for them. The blessings will happen as you speak them because they are the word of God.

In the Beatitudes, Matthew 5:3–11, the Lord Jesus Christ made it clear that we position ourselves to be blessed. Our attitudes are very important in this matter.

In Genesis 25:5-6, 11; the Bible declares, "And Abraham gave all that he had unto Isaac. But unto the sons of the concubines, which Abraham had, Abraham gave gifts, and sent them away from Isaac his son, while he yet lived, eastward, unto the east country. And it came to pass after the death of Abraham, that God blessed his son Isaac; and Isaac dwelt by the well Lahai-roi". God blessed Isaac because Isaac was the one who was set aside, or chosen, to be blessed. Once a person is blessed, the Lord guards that one combatively and makes sure that he or she is protected.

When Jacob stole Esau's blessings by disguising himself as Esau, Esau was very angry and decided to kill Jacob after the death of their father, Isaac. The Lord protected Jacob. Jacob fled to his Uncle Laban, who for many years planned evil against him in many ways—but Jacob prevailed over Laban. When Esau and Jacob met again, Jacob was afraid, but the Lord protected him yet again.

In Genesis 49:1–27, Jacob called his sons and blessed every one of them according to their characters. These blessings played an important part in their destinies.

Balak, king of the Moabites, sent a messenger to Balaam, the son of Beor, at Pethar, telling him to come and curse Israel. God quickly intervened; He appeared to Balaam in a dream (Numbers 22:8–12). God stopped Balaam from cursing Israel.

Balak said, "Come now therefore, I pray thee, curse me this people; for they are too mighty for me: peradventure I shall prevail, that we may smite them, and that I may drive them out of the land: for I wot that he whom thou blesses is blessed, and he whom thou cursest is cursed" (Number 22:6). We must not take blessings lightly. Once the word goes forth, it is very difficult to cancel it with curses.

Numbers 23:19–25 states, "God is not a man, that He should lie; neither the son of man, that he should repent: hath He said, and shall He not do it? Or hath He spoken, and shall He not make it good? Behold, I have received commandment to bless: and He hath blessed; and I cannot reverse it. He hath not beheld iniquity in Jacob, neither hath He seen perverseness in Israel: the Lord his God is with him, and the shout of a king is among them. God brought them out of Egypt; He hath as it were the strength of a unicorn. Surely there is no enchantment against Jacob, neither is there any divination against Israel: according to this time it shall be said of Jacob and of Israel, What hath God wrought! Behold, the people shall rise up as a great lion, and lift up himself as a young lion: he shall not lie down until he eat of the prey, and drink the blood of the slain. And Balak said unto Balaam, Neither curse them at all, nor bless them at all." Balak was frustrated at the power of the blessing upon Israel that was coming out Balaam's mouth. He commanded Balaam not to bless them or to curse them, as he had wanted earlier.

Blessing is visible. When God blesses a person, the people around that person will see that he or she is blessed. "And it came to pass at that time, that Abimelech and Phicol the chief captain of his host spake unto Abraham, saying, God is with thee in all that thou doest" (Genesis 21:22). The blessing of God on Abraham had become obvious for the people around him to acknowledge it.

Abimelech was the king of Gerar. He took Abraham's wife in Genesis 20:1–6. God intervened and stopped Abimelech from sleeping with Sarah; He revealed to Abimelech that Sarah was Abraham's wife, although Abraham himself had lied to the king that Sarah was his sister.

Abraham had been afraid the Philistines would kill him if they knew Sarah was his wife. When Abraham first arrived at Gerar, God had blessed him: "Now the Lord had said unto Abram, get thee out of thy country, and from thy kindred, and from thy father's house, unto a land that I will shew thee. And I will make of thee a great nation, and I will bless thee, and make thy name great; and thou shalt be a blessing. And I will bless them that bless thee, and curse him that curseth thee: and in thee shall all families of the earth be blessed" (Genesis 12:1–3).

God's blessing on Abraham has importance that affects the whole world to this day. Through Abraham, we have Jesus, and Jesus Christ, our Savior and Lord, has made us blessed.

Now I believe that most people here on earth have heard the gospel of Jesus Christ, which is a great blessing to all humanity. How do we know this? "Know ye therefore that they which are of faith, the same are the children of Abraham. And the scripture, foreseeing that God would justify the heathen through faith, preached before the gospel unto Abraham, saying, In thee shall all nations be blessed. So then they which be of faith are blessed with faithful Abraham. Christ hath redeemed us from the curse of the law, being made a curse for us: for it is written, Cursed is every one that hangeth on a tree" (Galatians 3:7–9, 13).

Blessing is a very important aspect of everyone's life. I suggest that mothers bless their children with a copy of this book for the sake of their future generations. Many people leave family heirlooms for the next generation.

Some people wear rings, necklaces, and other jewelry with pride because their grandmothers, fathers, grand-aunts, and other family members left these things to them as a legacy. Personally, I believe the best legacy anyone can leave for the next generation is the pronouncement of blessings on them.

Pastors can organize a pronouncing-of-blessings day, to bless their church members; it can be called a day of benediction, or any other name they choose. Grandfathers can also do the same, and bless their children. Fathers and mothers can do the same on Thanksgiving Day,

Christmas Day, or at family reunions. Blessing is the greatest legacy anyone can leave for their family.

This is not the exhaustive account of blessings in the word of God. There are still a plethora of blessings to be discovered in the Bible. Most of the scriptures are paraphrased to suit this format (blessings).

INTRODUCTION

Blessed are the poor in spirit for theirs is the kingdom of heaven: The Lord Jesus taught His disciples the Beatitudes so they could position themselves in a place of blessing. Blessings do not just happen; there is an attitude for blessing which we all must put on.

In Genesis 35:22, Reuben slept with Bilhah, his father's concubine. "And it came to pass, when Israel dwelt in that land, that Reuben went and lay with Bilhah his father's concubine: and Israel heard it. Now the sons of Jacob were twelve." This brought a great woe unto Reuben. When his father was blessing his children, his pronouncement on Reuben was not favorable.

It is very harsh, and even scary to read. He said, "Reuben, thou art my firstborn, my might and the beginning of my strength, the excellency of dignity, and the excellency of power. Unstable as water, thou shalt not excel, because thou wentest up to thy father's bed; then defiledst thou it: he went up to my couch" (Genesis 49:3–4). What a fearful pronouncement upon one's own son. Being the firstborn son of Jacob, Reuben would have been blessed, but his choices in life cost him this blessing (Genesis 35:22).

Blessing is something that we must desire for. You should desire to acquire it and, as a matter of fact, you must show that you want it through your lifestyle. Jacob knew what it meant to be blessed. He stole his brother Esau's blessings, which he desired aggressively (Genesis 27:1–29). When he encountered the angel of the Lord, he held onto the angel and refused to let go of the angel of the Lord, until the man blessed him.

"Blessed are the poor in spirit: for theirs is the kingdom of heaven" (Matthew 5:3). Jesus explained to the disciples what it meant to be poor in spirit. These days, many people are dabbling in the occult and joining cults in order to be furnished with unknown spirits, and witchcraft power. This is causing a lot of problems everywhere. People want to control their environment through the means of magic, and divination. In Revelation 17:14; the Word of God says, "These shall make war with the Lamb, and the Lamb shall overcome them: for he is Lord of lords, and King of kings: and they that are with him are called, and chosen, and faithful." People who are rich in spirit will not see the kingdom of heaven. "For without are dogs, and sorcerers, and whoremongers, and murderers, and idolaters, and whosoever loveth and maketh a lie" (Revelation 22:15). As Christians, the only spirit that we should be rich in is the Holy Spirit of God, and nothing else.

"Blessed are they that mourn: for they shall be comforted" (Matthew 5:4). The Lord always comforts those who mourn. "Blessed be God, even the Father of our Lord Jesus Christ, the Father of mercies, and the God of all comfort; Who comforteth us in all our tribulation, that we may be able to comfort them which are in any trouble, by the comfort wherewith we ourselves are comforted of God" (2 Corinthians 1:3–4). God comforts us so that we can, in turn, comfort those who are going through problems. It is a blessing to receive comfort from family and friends when one is in trouble.

"Blessed are the meek: for they shall inherit the earth" (Matthew 5:5). Meekness is defined in Webster's Dictionary as enduring injury with patience, without resentment; that is submissive, not violent or strong. We must be totally dependent on the Holy Spirit and on the Lord, especially when dealing with people who abuse or take advantage of our Christianity.

"Blessed are they which do hunger and thirst after righteousness: for they shall be filled" (Matthew 5:6). Walking with the Lord, we face daily choices in life. Some choices have to do with friends, our jobs, even our families. When you begin to grow in the Lord, you will start to give up certain things. Your family members might then begin to persecute you. For example, you might decide to give up drinking alcohol because if you really want to grow in the Lord, the thirst for holiness in your heart will begin to show for all to see. The first people who will notice the changes will be your own family members and then your friends—people who are very close to you. If they are not in agreement with you, there will be immediate friction. At that point, you will be faced with a choice. Which path will you choose?

"Blessed are the merciful: for they shall obtain mercy" (Matthew 5:7). The Lord will show mercy to anyone who himself shows mercy. Jesus taught the parable of the servants in Matthew 18:22–35. He compared the kingdom of heaven to a certain king who took account of his servants. One of the servants owed him ten thousand talents but could not pay the king. The king was supposed to sell the servant, his wife, and his children to pay for the amount owed, but he did not. Instead, he forgave the servant. When the servant departed from the kings presence, he saw a fellow servant who owed him one hundred pence; he grabbed the other servant, and demanded his money. The fellow servant begged for more time to pay the debt. The servant who had been forgiven so much by the king did not heed his fellow's pleas but sent him to prison until he was able to pay the hundred pence. All the other servants, who had witnessed how the king had forgiven the debt of ten thousand talents, intimated to the king what had happened. The king called the servant, and reprimanded him for his wickedness. Why couldn't he have forgiven his fellow servant for a small amount owed, when he himself had been forgiven a large amount? The king was angry; he ordered for the servant to be sent to prison until he could pay what he owed. Jesus said, "So likewise shall my heavenly Father do also unto you, if ye from your hearts forgive not everyone his brother their trespasses" (Matthew 18:35). Also, in the Lord's prayer, He said, "And forgive us our sins; for we also forgive every one that is indebted to us. And lead us not into temptation; but deliver us from evil" (Luke 11:4). The Scriptures make it plain and clear that our being forgiven depends upon how we ourselves forgive. Likewise, our being blessed also depends on our setting ourselves in a position to be blessed.

"Blessed are the pure in heart: for they shall see God" (Matthew 5:8). The condition of our hearts will determine whether we will see God or not. The Lord demands that we clear our hearts of all that besets us. Psalm 24:3–5 states, "Who shall ascend into the hill of the Lord? Or who shall stand in His holy place? He that hath clean hands, and a pure heart; who hath not lifted up his soul unto vanity, nor sworn deceitfully. He shall receive the blessing from the Lord, and righteousness from the God of his salvation." The purity of our hearts is the key.

"Blessed are the peacemakers: for they shall be called the children of God" (Matthew 5:9). Operating in peace is a major factor in receiving blessing from God. The Lord is a God of peace, therefore His children must be imitators of Him. The Bible calls Him the Prince of Peace in Isaiah 9:6: "For unto us a child is born, unto us a Son is given: and the government shall be upon His shoulder: and His name shall be called Wonderful, Counselor, The mighty God, The everlasting Father, The Prince of Peace." Our lives here on earth must imitate Christ's; otherwise, we deceive ourselves.

"Blessed are they which are persecuted for righteousness' sake: for theirs is the kingdom of heaven" (Matthew 5:10). Persecution sometimes occurs in our own families when we give our lives totally to the Lord, but we ought to bless people, and not curse them. The Lord said we should bless our enemies. We belong to a kingdom whose King is the King of heaven, the Lord Jesus Christ Himself; we should try not to be offended when we are persecuted here on earth. We have a better home in heaven, Hallelujah!

"Blessed are ye, when men shall revile you, and persecute you, and shall say all manner of evil against you falsely, for my sake. Rejoice, and be exceeding glad: for great is your reward in heaven: for so persecuted they the prophets which were before you" (Matthew 5:11–12). The Lord Jesus was accused falsely because He stood for the truth. If you are His, and you stand for the truth, you will be persecuted, too. Men will lie about you and misquote the things you say, but you have an advocate who is greater than everything that men would level against you.

The Lord has so many blessings in store for His people. We must try to live holy lives unto Him. "These things I have spoken unto you, that in me ye might have peace. In the world ye shall have tribulation: but be of good cheer; I have overcome the world" (John 16:33). We overcome the world in Christ Jesus, and in Christ alone. Be blessed, beloved.

Chapter 1

PRONOUNCING THE BLESSINGS OF THE BIBLE

Say these blessings out loud.

1. God bless you and make you fruitful and multiply you to fill the earth and subdue it, and to have dominion over the fish of the sea, and over the fowl of the air, and over every living thing that moves upon the earth (Gen. 1:28).
2. May God breathe into you His breath of life to renew your health daily (Gen. 2:7).
3. In your endeavors, may you gravitate to the tree of life always (Gen. 2:17).
4. May the Lord cause you to find the right life partner (Gen. 2:24).

5. May you find grace in the eyes of the Lord (Gen. 6:8).

6. May the Lord preserve you and your entire household (Gen. 7:1).

7. May disaster never find you, may the Lord remember you always, and may He send a powerful wind to blow away all your problems (Gen. 8:1).

8. May God bless you and your descendants, and may He cause you to be fruitful and multiply and replenish the earth (Gen 9:1).

9. May every place you tread be blessed thus: He will bless your environment. May the dread of you fall upon every beast of the land, every bird of the air, everything that creeps upon the ground, and all the fish of the sea (Gen. 9:2).

10. May He give you supply of food, vegetables, plants, and all kinds of food and green herbs (Gen. 9:3).

11. May God send a rainbow in the midst of your clouds (Gen. 9:13).

12. May the Lord bless and enlarge you (Gen. 9:27).

13. May you be mighty before the Lord (Gen. 10:8).

14. The Lord will make you a great nation. He will bless you and make your name great and you will be a blessing. The Lord will bless those who bless you and curse those who curse you and bless all those around you (Gen. 12:2–3).

15. May the Lord intervene in your circumstances and difficulties as He did for Abraham when Pharaoh took his wife Sarah (Gen. 12:17–20).

16. The Lord will cause you to be enlarged northwards, southwards, eastwards, and westwards (Gen. 13:14).

17. May the Lord multiply your seed as the dust of the earth (Gen. 13:16).

18. Blessed be you by God, Most High, Creator of heaven and earth. Blessed be God Most High, who delivered your enemies into your hand (Gen. 14:19-20).

19. May the Lord give you long life (Gen. 15:15).

20. May the Lord be your shield and abundant compensation and may your reward be exceedingly great (Gen 15:14)

21. The Lord will cause you to live long. May you never be part of a decision that would jeopardize your future or the future of your

descendants. May the Lord help you to walk habitually before Him and be protected (Gen 16:2).

22. May the Lord multiply you exceedingly. May the Lord change your name and give you a new name. May He cause you to walk in habitual relationship with Him. May the Lord cause the people around you to be in one accord with you as you serve Him in Spirit and in truth. May the Lord cause you to be fruitful in your old age (Gen. 17:1–15).

23. The Lord will cause others to be blessed through you; He will make you great and mighty, for He has chosen you as His own. He will direct you and help you teach your children to do what is just and righteous so that the Lord may bring the blessings He has promised you to pass (Gen. 18:16–19).

24. You will not be destroyed with the wicked people; the Lord will single you out and set intercessors to intercede on your behalf until your purpose is fulfilled. No one will snatch what belongs to you. You will possess your possessions (Gen 18:23-33).

25. You will receive compensation from all who have wronged you (Gen. 20:14).

26. May the Lord provide water in your wilderness (Gen. 21:19).

27. May the Lord bless you in all things (Gen. 24:1).

28. May the Lord show kindness to you at all times (Gen. 24:12).

29. May the Lord lead you in the right way always (Gen. 24:26–27).

30. May people see the blessing of God on you, and do you good, and even provide for you in a very special way (Gen. 24:31–32).

31. You are blessed, (*say name here*); be the mother/ father of thousands of millions, and let your seed possess the gates of those who hate them (Gen. 24:60).

32. May God bless your children (Gen. 25:11).

33. May the Lord bless you and your seed and give you an inheritance (Gen. 26:2–4).

34. When you sow, may the Lord cause you to receive a hundredfold, and may the Lord bless you and cause you to wax great, and go forward until you become very great (Gen. 26:12–13).

35. May the Lord be with you, bless you, and multiply you and your seed forever (Gen. 26:24).

36. May God give you the dew of heaven and the fatness of the earth, and plenty of corn and wine. May people serve you and nations bow down to you; be lord over other brethren. Cursed be everyone who curses you and blessed be everyone who blesses you (Gen. 27:28–29).

37. May God Almighty bless you and make you fruitful, and multiply you that you may be a multitude of people. May He give the blessing of Abraham to you and to your seed, and may He give you an inheritance (Gen. 28:3–4).

38. Your seed shall be as the dust of the earth and you shall spread abroad to the west and to the east and to the north and to the south; people will be blessed through you. The Lord be with you wherever you go. The Lord will not leave you until He has done all these things in your life (Gen. 28:14–15).

39. May your blessings be contagious. Your associates will see that the Lord has blessed them for your sake (Gen. 30:27).

40. May the Lord be good to you and make your descendants as the sand of the sea (Gen. 32:12).

41. The Lord will make you a prince; He will give you power with Himself and power with men. He will cause you to prevail and be blessed (Gen 32:28–29).

42. You will never become a victim of circumstance. The Lord will always deliver you and your descendants from every molestation of the enemy. The Lord will answer your prayers, and when you are in any form of distress, He will be with you. No one will harm you. May the Lord give you a new name. Kings and great men will be among your descendants. May the Lord deliver you from every plot of the enemy, in Jesus' name (Gen. 33:1–15).

43. The terror of God will be upon your enemies so that they will not be able to harm you (Gen. 35:5).

44. May the Lord be with you and may you prosper in every situation in which you find yourself (Gen. 39:2).

45. May the Lord bless you, make all that you do prosper, and cause you to find grace in the

sight of your superiors. When it is time for your promotion, may you be promoted accordingly. May the Lord bless people around you (Gen. 39:3–6).

46. May the blessing of the Lord be on you in the house and in the field (Gen. 39:5).

47. The Lord will intervene on your behalf in all areas of your life. Whatever belongs to you will not be taken from you in any way (Gen. 20:3–7).

48. The Lord will bring His promise to your life. The Lord will visit you even in your old age, even at the set time of which He has spoken (Gen. 21:1–2).

49. The Lord will give you the ability to pass all your tests; He will provide you with strength and materials for sacrifice (Gen. 22:1–7).

50. The Lord will send His angel ahead of you and see to it that you will be successful in all your endeavors. He will help you accomplish your purpose (Gen. 22:10–12).

51. May the Lord bless you to possess the gates of your enemies, as you obey His voice He

will cause people to be blessed through your obedience (Gen. 22:15–18).

52. May the Lord cause people to notice your gifts and bring you before great men and kings (Gen. 41:14–15).

53. May the Lord elevate you to the highest heights (Gen. 41:41–44).

54. May the Lord make you first on the list of honor. In the time of famine, the Lord will preserve you and be with you (Gen. 46:2–4).

55. May God bless you as He did Ephraim and Manasseh (Gen. 48:20).

56. Your hands shall be on the necks of your enemies; your father's children shall bow before you (Gen. 49:8).

57. You will be a fruitful bough by a well whose branches run over a wall. Your bough will stay strong and the arm of your hand will be made strong by the hand of the Almighty God of Jacob (Gen. 49:22–24).

58. You will be helped by the God of Israel and by the Almighty, who shall bless you with blessings of heaven above, blessings of the deep that lies

under, and blessings of the breasts and of the womb (Gen. 49:25).

59. The blessings of your Father have prevailed above the blessings of my progenitors unto the utmost bound of the everlasting hills; they shall be on the head of (*say name here*) and on the crown of the head of him that was separated from his brothers (Gen 49:25–26).

60. May the Lord cause you to increase abundantly, and multiply, and wax exceedingly mighty, to fill the land you are in (Ex. 1:7).

61. May God deal well with you and cause you to multiply and wax very mighty (Ex. 1:20).

62. The Lord intervenes always on your behalf. In times of trouble, may the Lord intervene and find you a deliverer (Ex. 2:9–10).

63. May you have vivid encounters with God that will bring a transformation in your life. May the Lord fight all your battles and defeat your enemies (Ex. 3:3–5).

64. May the Lord work wonders in your life. May He give you favor even with your enemies (Ex. 3:19–21).

65. May the Lord put a division between you and your enemies (Ex. 8:23).

66. May the Lord cause all plagues to pass over you. You will not be affected by any plague of the land (Ex. 12:12).

67. When He sees the blood, He will pass over you (Ex. 12:23).

68. The Lord will put none of these diseases upon you; He is the Lord your healer. (Exodus 15:26)

69. May the Lord give you the supply of food at all times (Ex. 16:4).

70. The Lord will always feed you (Ex. 16:11–14).

71. May the Lord bring good counselors in your time of need just as He brought Jethro to Moses (Ex. 18:18–23).

72. May the Lord bear you on eagles' wings, and bring you out of trouble. Obey His voice, for He will make you a peculiar treasure (Ex. 19:4–6).

73. No one will attack or conquer your land when you appear before the Lord your God each year. The Lord will drive out the nations that stand in your way and He will enlarge your boundaries (Ex. 34:24).

74. May the Lord cause you to glow as you wait on Him and serve Him well (Ex. 34:29).

75. May the Lord give you special skills so that you will excel in all kinds of designs (Ex. 35:35).

76. May the Lord give you all that you will ever need to serve Him and serve Him well (Ex. 39:1–31).

77. May all your offerings be acceptable to the Lord God Almighty (Ex. 9:22–24).

78. May your land yield bumper crops for you to eat to your fill, and may you live securely in it (Lev. 25:19).

79. May the Lord give you peace in the land so you will be able to sleep without fear (Lev. 26:6).

80. The Lord will look favorably upon you and multiply your people and fulfill His covenant with you (Lev. 26:9).

81. May God bless you with surplus crops so that you will have to get rid of leftovers from the previous year (Lev. 26:10).

82. The Lord bless you, and keep you: The Lord make His face shine upon you, and be gracious unto you: The Lord lift up His countenance upon you, and give you peace. (Num. 6:24-26)

83. No misfortune is in sight for (*say name here*); no trouble is in store for Israel. For the Lord your God is with you. He has been proclaimed your King. God has brought you out of Egypt (the world). He is like a strong ox.

84. No curse can touch (*say name here*). No sorcery has any power against (*say name here*). For it will be said of (*say name here*) that the Lord does wonders on your behalf (Num. 23:21–23).

85. You will be blessed above all nations of the earth. None of your men or women will be childless, just as all your livestock will bear their young (Deut. 7.14).

86. And the Lord will protect you from all sickness; He will not let you suffer from the terrible diseases you knew in Egypt, but will bring them all upon your enemies (Deut. 7:15).

87. The Lord your God will bless you as He has promised. You will lend money to many nations but you will never borrow. You will rule many nations but they will not rule over you (Deut. 15:6).

88. The Lord will give you bountiful harvests, and bless all your work (Deut. 16:15).

89. The Lord your God will exalt you above all the nations of the world. You will experience all these blessings if you obey the Lord your God (Deut 26:19).

90. Blessed shall you be in the city, and blessed shall you be in the field. Blessed shall be the fruit of your body, and the fruit of your ground, and the fruit of your cattle, the increase of your kine, and the flock of your sheep. (Deut 28:3-4).

91. Blessed shall be your basket, and your store. Blessed shall you be when you come in, and blessed shall you be when you go out. The Lord shall cause your enemies that rise up against you to be smitten before your face: they shall come out against you one way, and flee before you seven ways (Deut 28:5-7).

92. The Lord shall command the blessing upon you in your storehouses, and in all that you set your hand unto; and he shall bless you in the land which the Lord your God gives you. The Lord will establish you a holy people unto Himself. All people of the earth shall see that

you are called by the name of the Lord, and they shall be afraid of you. (Deut 28:8-10).

93. The Lord will make you plenteous in goods, in the fruit of your body. And in the fruit of your cattle and in the fruit of your ground (Deut 28:11)

94. The Lord open unto you His good treasure, the heaven to give rain unto your land in its season. The Lord bless all the work of your hand, and you shall lend unto many nations, and you shall not borrow. The Lord will make you the head, and not the tail, and you shall be above only, and you not be beneath (Deut. 28:12-13).

95. The Lord your God will cleanse your heart and the hearts of all your descendants, so that you will love Him with all your heart and soul. The Lord will inflict curses on your enemies and persecutors (Deut. 30:6–7).

96. The Lord your God will make you successful in everything you do. He will give you many children and numerous livestock and make your fields produce abundant harvest, for the Lord will delight in being good to you as He

was to your ancestors. The Lord your God will delight in you if you obey His voice and keep His commands and laws. Turn to the Lord your God and He will neither fail you nor forsake you (Deut. 30:9–10).

97. The Lord will hear the cry of (*say name here*) and bring him/her again to his/her people. Give you strength to defend your cause. May the Lord help you against your enemies (Deut 33:7).

98. The Lord will crush the loins of your enemies; He will strike down your foes so they never rise again. The Lord will surround you continuously and preserve you from every harm. May your land be blessed by the Lord with the choice gifts of rain from the heavens, and water from beneath the earth, with riches that grow each month, with the finest crops of the ancient mountains, with the abundance from the everlasting hills, with the best gifts of the earth and its fullness, and the favor of the One who appeared in the burning bush. May these blessings rest on your head. May you prosper in your expectations abroad (Deut 33:11).

99. May you prosper at home. You will benefit from the riches of the sea and the hidden treasures of the sand. The Lord will enlarge your territory. May the Lord give you His best of everything (Deut 33:19).

100. You will be rich in favor and full of the Lord's blessing. May you be blessed above others, may your feet be bathed in olive oil, may your strength match the length of your days (Deut 33:24-25).

101. The eternal God will be your refuge and His everlasting arms are under you. He will thrust out the enemy before you so that you will live in safety, prosperity and security (Deut 33:27-28).

102. The Lord is your shield and the sword of your excellence. Your enemies will bow low before you, and you will trample on them, and their high places. (Deut. 33:29).

103. May your eyes not dim, nor your natural force ever diminish (abate) (Deut. 34:7).

104. As you serve the Lord, no one will be able to stand their ground against you as long as you live, for the Lord will be with you. He will not fail or abandon you (Josh 1:5).

105. As you study and meditate on the word of God day and night and obey His word, you will be successful in all your endeavors (Josh. 1:8).

106. The Lord will make you great in the eyes of all men so that they will know that the Lord is with you. The Lord will drive out your enemies from you. The Lord will make a way for you where there is no way (Josh. 3:7).

107. May the Lord cause your enemies to lose heart. May He paralyze them with fear (Josh. 5:1–15).

108. May no accursed thing ever be found in your possession (Josh. 7:1-26).

109. May the Lord remove the spirit of fear and discouragement from you (Josh. 8:1).

110. May the Lord give you bounty (Josh. 8:27).

111. May the Lord remove every form of deception from you. The Lord will cause the fear of you to fall upon anyone who plots to harm you (Josh. 9).

112. May the Lord give you rest on every side. No enemy should be able to stand against you, for the Lord will help you conquer all your enemies. May all the good promises that the

Lord has given you come to pass, in Jesus' name! (Josh 1:13)

113. May the Lord give you the ability to be faithful to Him, and to serve Him with all your heart, and all your soul (Josh. 1:15).

114. May the Lord drive away all your powerful enemies and cause you to put a thousand enemies to flight. May the Lord fight for you (Josh. 23:9).

115. The Lord will give you victory over enemies that fight against you (Josh. 24:8).

116. May the Lord give you peace all the days of your life (Judg. 3:30).

117. May the Lord throw all your enemies into panic, and chase them away from you. Their entire plot against you will be upon their own heads (Judg. 4:15).

118. May the Lord do unto your enemies as He did unto Sisera, captain of Jabin's army (Judg. 4:21).

119. May those who love you rise like the sun at its full strength (Judg. 5:31).

120. May you be filled with the Spirit of the Lord to do as the Lord has destined you to do, and accomplish it. (Judges 6:34)

121. May the Lord help you accomplish your purpose, and may you honor Him when that purpose is accomplished. May the honor be given to God, and not to man (Judg. 8:5–27).

122. May you always serve the Lord and never deviate from His precepts and ordinances. May the Lord rescue you from all your enemies (Judg. 10:6–17).

123. May you live to possess your rightful inheritance (Judg. 11:9–10).

124. You will not be a victim of circumstances (Judg. 11:36–44).

125. May the Lord give you your heart's desire. May He bless you all the days of your life. May the Spirit of the Lord take hold of you all the days of your life (Judg. 13:24–25).

126. May the Lord give you physical strength to overcome your enemies (Judg. 14:5–6).

127. May the Lord quench your thirst at all times (Judg. 15:19).

128. May neither you nor your descendants ever become victims of Delilah (Judg. 16:11–20).

129. May you be victorious all your life, even in your last hour (Judg. 16:26–30).

130. May the Lord bless you with the security of marriage (Ruth 1:9).

131. May you find a Ruth in your life (Ruth 1:16–17).

132. May the Lord God of Israel, under whose wings you have come to take refuge, reward you fully (Ruth 2:12).

133. In the course of your life, may the Lord cause you to meet your Boaz, in Jesus' name (Ruth 2:15).

134. (*For newlyweds*) May the Lord make the woman who is now coming to your house be like Rachel and Leah, from whom all the nation of Israel descended. May you be great in the entire world. May the Lord give you descendants by this woman who will be like Perez, son of Tamar, and Judah (Ruth 4:11–12).

135. May the Lord bless you, and may He never leave you without a kinsman (Ruth 4:14).

136. May the Lord bring a great restoration in your life (Ruth 4:15–17).

137. May the Lord God of Israel grant all the requests you ask of Him (1 Sam. 1:17).

138. May the Lord give you favor with God, and favor with men (1 Sam. 2:26).

139. The Lord will bless your family, and your descendants will be priests and kings forever (1 Sam. 2:35).

140. When the voice of the Lord becomes scarce, you will hear His voice when He speaks (1 Sam. 3:1–14).

141. May the Lord be with you and cause you to grow. May the Lord appear to you, and lead you in all your ways (1 Sam. 3:19–21).

142. May the Lord subdue your enemies under your feet (1 Sam. 7:13).

143. May the Lord look down on you with mercy and send you a deliverer (1 Sam. 9:16).

144. May the Lord honor you as you live to honor Him at all times (1 Sam. 10:22–27).

145. May the Spirit of the Lord be upon you, and transform you into a new person (1 Sam. 10:6).

146. May God give you a band of men whose hearts the Lord has touched to become

your companions and help you fulfill your assignments (1 Sam. 10:26).

147. May the Lord give you the ability to solve your family problems (1 Sam. 10:9–14).

148. May the Lord anoint you, and cause evil spirits to depart from your presence (1 Sam. 16:23).

149. May the Lord make you victorious over all your enemies as David was victorious over Goliath (1 Sam. 17:48–50).

150. May the Lord put the fear of you upon your enemies (1 Sam. 18:12).

151. May the Lord give you wisdom to behave yourself wisely in all your ways, and may the Lord be with you (1 Sam. 18:14).

152. Let the Lord put love in the hearts of the people you operate with, on a daily basis (1 Sam. 18:16).

153. May any conspiracy against you be exposed to you, in Jesus' name (1 Sam. 19:1–2).

154. May you escape every trap of your enemies (1 Sam. 19:10–18).

155. May God give you good friends like David and Jonathan (1 Sam. 20:2–42).

156. When the Lord delivers your enemies into your hands, may you do no evil (1 Sam. 24:4, 10).

157. May the Lord cause you to meet with people who will give you divine counsel, so that you never fall into trouble (1 Sam. 25:25).

158. May the Lord deliver you from all tribulations (1 Sam. 26:24).

159. If you lose anything, may the Lord help you recover all (1 Sam. 30:18).

160. May the Lord cause you to lack nothing (1 Sam. 30:19).

161. As you do the will of the Lord, may He bless you, and all your household as He blessed Obededom the Gittite (2 Sam. 6:11).

162. Now let it please the Lord to bless you. May He Bless your house so that it may continue forever and ever (2 Sam. 7:29).

163. May the Lord preserve you, wherever you go (2 Sam 8:1–8).

164. May all people bless you with gold, silver, and brass (2 Sam. 8:10).

165. May the Lord cause people to show you kindness all your life (2 Sam. 9:7).

166. May the Lord turn the counsel of your enemies into foolishness (2 Sam. 15:31).

167. May the Lord give you favor, and supply all that you need at the time of your need(2 Sam. 17:27–29).

168. May the Lord cause your enemies to be like Absalom, who rise up against you only to fall into their own deceit (2 Sam. 18:28–33).

169. May the Lord send you a rescuer whenever you are in trouble (2 Sam. 21:1:7).

170. You shall be as the light of the morning at sunrise on a cloudless day, as the tender grass springing out of the earth after it has rained (2 Sam. 23:4).

171. May you receive the Lord's rich blessings, and may God give you a descendant to inherit all your blessings (1 Kings 2:45).

172. May the Lord give you a wise and understanding mind such as no one has ever had. May He bestow upon you riches, honor, and long life (1 Kings 3:12–13).

173. May the Lord give you wisdom to administer justice, and to be effective in your calling (1 Kings 3:28).

174. May God provide for you as He provided for Solomon (1 Kings 4:22).

175. May the wisdom of Solomon be extended to you so that you can achieve your purpose (1 Kings 4:29).

176. May the Lord make you unique in the gift that He has given you, so that it will be a blessing to humanity (1 Kings 4:34).

177. May God give you good friends like Hiram, king of Tyre, to help you achieve your purpose (1 Kings 5:1–12).

178. May you be able to fulfill your assignment in the time that God has given you (1 Kings 6:2–38).

179. May you accomplish your purpose and assignment with excellence and dignity (1 Kings 7:1–51).

180. May God give an inheritance to your children (1 Kings 8:25).

181. May the Lord hear you when you call (1 Kings 8:28–29).

182. May the eye of the Lord be upon whatever you do perpetually (1 Kings 9:4).

183. May God help your children, and ancestors keep the statutes of God eternally (1 Kings 9:6).

184. May the Lord, in your lifetime send you your own Queen of Sheba, to bring you substances of gold, and every precious stone (1 Kings 10:10).

185. May God give you all kinds of blessings of gold and precious stones, and the best of everything from all over the world (1 Kings 10:14–15).

186. May you never fall victim to circumstance, and may the Lord help you make the right choices in life. Let your heart be perfect; serve the Lord in true humility, and faithfulness (1 Kings 11:1–10).

187. Let the fire of God fall whenever you request it (1 Kings 18:38).

188. May the Lord grant you divine acceleration so that you will be swifter on foot, than those riding chariots (1 Kings 18:46).

189. May God deliver you from the hands of any Jezebel (1 Kings 19:1–3).

190. May the Lord give you a great, and faithful successor (1 Kings 19:19–21).

191. May the Lord give you a double portion of all that you desire (2 King 2:9–10).

192. May God help you pay all your debts, and supply all your needs (2 Kings 4:7).

193. May the Lord reward you for all you do for Him, and the men and women in the Lord's vineyard (2 Kings 4:16).

194. May the Lord heal you of every disease, in Jesus' name (2 Kings 5:14).

195. May the Lord reveal to you all that your enemies plan against you (2 Kings 6:8–11).

196. May you be protected at all times and may the Lord send His angels to protect you any time you are in danger (2 Kings 6:16–17).

197. The Lord will set blindness upon the enemy so that they may not see you to harm you (2 Kings 6:18–20).

198. May the Lord caution you when harm is near (2 Kings 6:32–33).

199. May the Lord restore unto you all the things you have lost (2 Kings 8:6).

200. For your sake, may the Lord not destroy your family (2 Kings 8:19).

201. May the Lord give you a great zeal for Him, in Jesus' name (2 Kings 10:16).

202. Whenever there is calamity, or pestilence near you, may the Lord send a deliverer to deliver you, and to preserve your life from any untimely death (2 Kings 11:2–3).

203. May the Lord preserve your life from evil people, and help you to possess your possessions (2 Kings 11:11–14).

204. You shall fear the Lord God, and He shall deliver you out of the hand of all your enemies (2 Kings 17:39).

205. May the Lord help you to remove every abominable thing from your life (2 Kings 18:4).

206. May you cleave to the Lord, and never depart from serving Him, in Jesus' name (2 Kings 18:6).

207. May the Lord be with you and cause you to prosper, wherever you go (2 Kings 18:7).

208. May the Lord send you people who will stand with you, and be loyal to you, as you will be to them (1 Chron. 12:17–22).

209. May the Lord bless you as you take good care of the things of God (1 Chron. 13:14).

210. May the Lord provide you your own Hiram, king of Tyre, to bring you all that you need to fulfill your destiny (1 Chron. 14:1).

211. May the Lord bring a confirmation to all your assignments (1 Chron. 14:2).

212. May the Lord bring the fear of you upon all the nations (1 Chron. 14:17).

213. May the Lord's blessings be established in the lives of you, and your family for ever as you serve Him faithfully (1 Chron. 17:26–27).

214. May the Lord give you victory over all your enemies (1 Chron. 20:8).

215. May the Lord God cause your enemies to make peace with you (1 Chron. 21:9–10).

216. The Lord God will be with you. He will not fail you nor forsake you until all your work in the services of the house of the Lord are completed (1 Chron. 28:20).

217. May the Lord God be with you, and magnify you exceedingly (2 Chron. 1:1).

218. May God show great mercy to you and to your descendants (2 Chron. 1:8).

219. May God give you wisdom, knowledge, riches, wealth, and honor (2 Chron. 2:12).

220. May the Lord bless you as He blessed Solomon (2 Chron. 9:13).

221. May people seek audience with you to hear your words of wisdom (2 Chron. 9:23).

222. May the Lord bless you, and give you rest on every side, and in everything you do (2 Chron. 14:7).

223. May the Lord bless you, and cause your voice to be heard, and let your prayer come up to His dwelling place even unto heaven (2 Chron. 30:27)

224. The Lord will be a wall of fire round about you. (Zech. 2:5a)

225. May the Lord cause you to succeed in everything you do (2 Chron. 32:30).

226. May all you need be granted you as the hand of the Lord is upon you (Ezra 7:6).

227. May the Lord extend mercy unto you before the king and his counselors. May He strengthen you with His mighty hand that is upon you (Ezra 7:27–28).

228. The gracious hand of our God be on you, and everyone that seek Him (Ezra 8:22).

229. May the hand of the Lord be on you and protect you from enemies, and bandits along the way (Ezra 8:31).

230. May the God of heaven give you success (Neh. 2:20).

231. May God give you faithful men who fear Him, to help you (Neh. 7:2).

232. May the Lord cause you to obtain favor in the sight of all who look upon you (Est. 2:15).

233. May the Lord give you light, gladness, joy, and honor (Est. 8:16).

234. What you decide on will be done, and light will shine upon your ways (Job 22:28).

235. As you delight in the law of the Lord and meditate on His word He shall make you to be like a tree planted by the rivers of water; your leaves shall not wither and whatsoever you do you shall prosper (Ps. 1:2–3).

236. Let the light of the face of the Lord shine upon you (Ps. 4:6).

237. May the Lord make the nations of the world your inheritance (Ps. 2:8).

238. May the Lord hear you when you call (Ps. 4:3).

239. May the Lord put more gladness in your heart than there was when there was corn and wine in abundance (Ps. 4:7).

240. May the Lord bless you and surround you with His favor as with a shield (Ps. 5:12).

241. The Lord will be a refuge in times of trouble (Ps. 9:9).

242. Let the Lord deal bountifully with you (Ps. 13:6).

243. May the Lord keep you as the apple of His eye and hide you in the shadow of His wings from the wicked who assail you (Ps. 17:8–9).

244. May the Lord deliver you from your strong enemy, and from those who hate you (Ps. 18:17).

245. May the Lord bring you into a large place because He delights in you (Ps. 18:19).

246. Let the Lord reward you according to your righteousness, according to the cleanness of your hands in His sight (Ps. 18:24).

247. May the Lord turn your darkness into light (Ps. 18:28).

248. By God, you will run through troops, and by God, you will leap over walls (Ps. 18:29).

249. May the Lord gird you with strength and make your way perfect (Ps. 18:32).

250. May the Lord give you a shield of salvation; let His right hand hold you up, and may His gentleness make you great (Ps. 18:35).

251. May the Lord answer you when you are in distress. May the name of the God of Jacob protect you. May he send you help from the sanctuary, and grant you support from Zion. May He remember all your sacrifices, and accept your offerings. May He give you the desires of your heart, and make all your plans succeed (Ps. 20:1–4).

252. May the Lord grant all your requests (Ps. 20:5).

253. May the Lord give you your heart's desire, and may He not withhold the request of your lips (Ps. 21:2).

254. May the Lord grant you length of days, forever and ever (Ps. 21:4).

255. May the Lord surely grant you eternal blessings, and make you glad with the joy of His presence (Ps. 21:6).

256. The Lord is your shepherd; you shall want nothing (Ps. 23:1).

257. Surely goodness and mercy shall follow you all the days of your life (Ps. 23:6).

258. You will spend your days in prosperity, and your descendants will inherit the land (Ps. 25:13).

259. The Lord give you strength, and may the Lord bless you with peace (Ps. 29:11).

260. The Lord has turned your mourning into dancing; He has put off your sackcloth, and girded you with gladness (Ps. 30:11).

261. May the Lord's unfailing love surround you as you trust in Him (Ps. 31:10).

262. May the Lord deliver you from death, and keep you alive in famine (Ps. 33:19).

263. May God's unfailing love rest upon you according as you hope in Him (Ps 33:22).

264. May the Lord bless you to inherit the land (Ps. 37:22).

265. Though you stumble, you will not fall, for the Lord will uphold you with His hand (Ps. 37:24).

266. Your children will be blessed (Ps. 37:26).

267. May the Lord put a new song in your mouth, even praise. Many shall see it and fear; they shall trust in the Lord (Ps. 40:3).

268. May the Lord withhold not His tender mercies from you. Let His loving kindness, and truth continually preserve you (Ps. 40:11).

269. The Lord will protect you, and preserve your life. He will bless you in the land, and will not surrender you to the desire of your foes (Ps. 41:2).

270. When God restores the fortunes of His people, let Jacob rejoice, and Israel be glad. May God restore your fortune, in Jesus' name (Ps. 53:6).

271. May the Lord deliver you out of all your troubles, and cause your eye to see His desire upon your enemies (Ps. 54:7).

272. May the Lord bring you to the place of abundance (Ps. 66:12).

273. May God be gracious unto you, and bless you, and make His face shine upon you (Ps. 67:1).

274. May the people praise God, and let the land yield its harvest, and God will bless them, and all the ends of the earth will fear Him (Ps. 67:5–7).

275. Blessed be the Lord, who daily loads you with benefits (Ps. 68:19).

276. May the God of Israel give power, and strength to you (Ps. 68:35).

277. May the Lord rescue you from oppression, and violence for your blood is precious in His sight. He will cause you to live long. May He cause you to receive gold from Sheba (Ps. 72:13–14).

278. May the Lord satisfy you early with mercy, so that you may rejoice and be glad (Ps. 90:14).

279. No evil will befall thee; neither shall any plague come near your dwelling (Ps. 91:10).

280. May the Lord satisfy you with long life, and show you His salvation (Ps. 91:16).

281. May the Lord cause you to flourish like the palm tree, and to grow like the cedar in Lebanon (Ps. 92:12).

282. You will still bring forth fruit in your old age; you will be fat, and flourish (Ps. 92:14).

283. May the Lord bless you and cause your number to increase greatly (Ps. 107:38).

284. The Lord will extend your mighty scepter from Zion; you will rule in the midst of your enemies (Ps. 110:2).

285. Your troops will be willing on your day of battle. Arrayed in Holy Majesty from the womb of the

dawn, you will receive the dew of your youth (Ps. 110:3).

286. The Lord will increase you more and more, you and your children (Ps. 115:14).

287. You are blessed of the Lord, which made heaven, and earth (Ps. 115:15).

288. Blessed are you who fear the Lord, who walk in His ways. You will eat the fruit of your labor; blessing, and prosperity will be yours. Your wife/husband will be like a fruitful vine within your house. Your sons will be like olive shoots around your table (Ps.128:1–3).

289. May the Lord bless you from Zion all the days of your life. May you see the prosperity of Jerusalem, and may you live to see your children's children (Ps. 128:5–6).

290. The blessing of the Lord is upon you (Ps. 129:8).

291. May the Lord, the Maker of heaven, and earth bless you out of Zion (Ps. 134.3).

292. The Lord will perfect everything that concerns you (Ps. 138:8).

293. May the Lord cause your sons to be as plants grown up in their youth, and your daughters

as corner stones, polished like a palace (Ps. 144:12).

294. May your fountain be blessed, and may you rejoice with the wife of your youth (Prov 5:18).

295. The Lord will cause you to inherit substance, and will fill your treasures (Prov. 8:21).

296. The Lord bless you with wisdom, so that your days may be multiplied, and your years shall be increased (Prov. 9:11).

297. May your tabernacle flourish, in Jesus' name (Prov. 14:11).

298. There will be much treasure in your house (Prov. 15:6).

299. May you follow after righteousness, and mercy to find life, and honor (Prov. 21:21).

300. You will have good things in your possession (Prov. 28:10).

301. May your seed be great and your offspring as the grass of the earth (Job 5:25).

302. You will come to your grave in full age, like a shock of corn comes in its season (Job 5:26).

303. May the Lord reward you for all your good works (Job 7:2).

304. May the Lord fill your mouth with laughter, and your lips with rejoicing (Job 8:21).

305. They that hate you shall be clothed with shame, and the dwelling place of the wicked shall come to nought (Job 8:22).

306. May the Lord grant you life and favor. May He preserve your spirit (Job 10:12).

307. May the Lord show you the secrets of wisdom (Job 11:6).

308. May the Lord cause you to lift up your face without spot, so that you will be steadfast, and not fear (Job 11:15).

309. May the Lord cause your life to be clearer than the noonday, and may you shine as the morning (Job 11:17).

310. You will be secured. (Job 11:18a)

311. May the Lord give you rest (Job 11:18).

312. When you lie down, no one will make you afraid. Many shall solicit your favor (Job 11:19).

313. May the Lord give you long life, wisdom, and understanding (Job 12:12).

314. When you call, may the Lord answer you (Job 14:15).

315. May the Lord make you stronger and stronger, because you have clean hands (Job 17:9).

316. May the Lord fill your house with good things (Job 22:18).

317. May the Almighty be your defense; may you have plenty of silver (Job 22:25).

318. May the Lord hear your prayer as you pay your vows (Job 22:27).

319. When you decree a thing, may it be established unto you; may light shine upon your ways (Job 22:28).

320. May you be delivered according to the pureness of your hands (Job 22:30).

321. May the Lord be your light, when you walk through darkness (Job 29:3).

322. Let the secret of the Lord be upon your tabernacle (Job 29:4).

323. May your steps be washed with butter, and let the rock pour out rivers of oil on you (Job 29:6).

324. When people hear you, let them bless you, and let people acknowledge you, when they see you (Job 29:11).

325. Let righteousness clothe you, and let your judgment be as a robe, and a diadem (Job 29:14).

326. May your root spread out by the waters, and may dew lay all night upon your branches (Job 29:19).

327. May the Lord deliver your soul from going to the pit, and cause your life to see light (Job 33:30).

328. May the Lord restore unto you a double portion of all that you have ever lost (Job 42:12–13).

329. The Spirit of the Lord will rest upon you, the spirit of wisdom and understanding, the spirit of counsel and of power, the spirit of knowledge and of the fear of the Lord (Isa. 11:2).

330. The Lord will keep you in perfect peace as your mind is steadfast because you trust in Him (Isa. 26:3).

331. The Lord will bless you as you wait on Him (Isa. 30:18).

332. May the Lord keep you from the pit of destruction, and put all your sins behind His own back (Isa. 38:17).

333. May the Lord cause you to renew your strength as you wait on Him. You will soar on wings like eagles, you will run and not grow weary, you will walk, and not be faint (Isa. 40:31).

334. When you pass through the waters He will be with you. When you pass through the rivers, they will not sweep over you. When you walk through the fire, you will not be burned. The flames will not set you ablaze (Isa. 43:2).

335. See, the Lord has engraved you in His hands (Isa. 49:16).

336. The Lord will contend with those who contend with you, and He will save your children (Isa. 49:25).

337. Your light will break forth like dawn, your healing will quickly appear, then your righteousness will go before you. The glory of the Lord will be your rear guard. Then you shall call the Lord and He will answer you. You will cry for help and He will say, Here am I (Isa. 58:8–9).

338. Your light will rise in darkness, and your night will become like the noonday. The Lord will guide you always. He will satisfy your needs

in a sun-scorched land. He will strengthen your frame. You will be like a well-watered garden, like a spring whose waters never fail (Isa. 58:10–11).

339. He will cause you to ride on the heights of the land, and to feast on the inheritance of your father, Jacob (Isa. 58:14).

340. But blessed is the man who trusts in the Lord, whose confidence is in Him. He will be like a tree planted by the water that sends out its roots by the stream. It does not fear when heat comes; its leaves are always green. It has no worries in a year of drought and never fails to bear fruit (Jer. 17:8).

341. The Lord will bless you and bless your surroundings. He will send showers in season; there shall be showers of blessing. Your trees will yield their fruit and your ground will yield its crops. You will be secured in your land (Ezek. 34:25–27).

342. May God give you knowledge and understanding of all kinds of literature and learning (Dan. 5:12).

343. May the Lord revive and restore you, and cause you to live in His presence (Hos. 6:2).

344. Your hands will be lifted up in triumph over your enemies and all your foes will be destroyed (Mic. 5:9).

345. May the Lord bless you from this day on (Hag. 2:18).

346. May the Lord make you like His signet ring (Hag. 2:23).

347. The Lord will be the glory in the midst of you. (Zech 2:5b)

348. May the Lord open unto you the floodgate of heaven and pour out so much blessing that you will not have room enough to receive it (Mal. 3:10).

349. The Lord will rebuke the devourer for your sake. All nations will call you blessed, for yours will be a delightsome land, says the Lord Almighty (Mal. 3:12).

350. May the Lord make you become salt of the earth (Matt. 5:13).

351. Be the light of the world (Matt. 5:14).

352. From now on, all generations shall call you blessed (Luke 1:48).

353. May the Lord cause you to grow in wisdom and stature, and in favor with God and men (Luke 2:52).

354. From the fullness of His grace, may you receive one blessing after another (John 1:16).

355. May the Lord give you the holy and sure blessings promised David (Acts 13:34).

356. The Lord shows you kindness by giving you rain from heaven and crops in their seasons; He will provide you with plenty of food, and fill your hearts with joy (Acts 14:17).

357. May the God of hope fill you with all joy, and peace as you trust in Him so that you may overflow with hope, by the power of the Holy Spirit (Rom. 15:13).

358. And God is able to make all grace abound to you, so that in all things at all times, having all that you need, you will abound in every good work (2 Cor. 9:8).

359. God the Father has blessed you in heavenly realms with every spiritual blessing in Christ (Eph. 1:3).

360. You are no longer foreigners and aliens, but fellow citizens with God's people and members of God's household (Eph. 2:19).

361. May the Lord strengthen your heart so that you will be blameless, and holy in the presence of our God, and Father when our Lord Jesus comes with all His holy ones (1 Thess. 3:13).

362. Now may the Lord of peace Himself give you peace at all times, in every way (2 Thess. 3:16).

363. The grace of our Lord Jesus Christ be with you all (2 Thess. 3:18).

364. May you be in health and prosper as your soul prospers (3 John 1:2).

365. The Lord will never blot out your name from His book of life, but will acknowledge your name before the Father, and His angels (Rev. 3:5).

366. Finally, after all these, in the end, may you not be left out. May you be amongst the redeemed of the Lord. Saying, Hallelujah! Salvation and glory, and honor, and power, unto the Lord our God forever and ever and ever!!! (Rev 19:1)

Chapter 2

BLESSINGS FOR FINANCIAL BREAKTHROUGH

Malachi 3:10 says,

> Bring ye all the tithes into the storehouse,
> that there may be meat in mine house, and
> prove me now herewith, saith the Lord of
> hosts, if I will not open you the windows
> of heaven, and pour you out a blessing,
> that there shall not be room enough to
> receive it.

Luke 6:38 says,

> Give, and it shall be given unto you;
> good measure, pressed down, and shaken

together, and running over, shall men give into your bosom. For with the same measure that ye mete withal it shall be measured to you again.

2 Corinthians 9:6 says,

But this I say, he which soweth sparingly shall reap also sparingly; and he which soweth bountifully shall reap also bountifully.

God's financial blessing comes when we give to God. Therefore, give and God will bless you abundantly. Learn to be a giver, and believe the Lord will bless you.

Prayer:

> Lord Jesus, You became poor so that, through Your poverty, I might become rich.
> Father, I ask for a financial blessing in my life.
> From today, I receive financial blessing in the name of Jesus.
> I walk in financial abundance, in Jesus' name.

- ➤ I have an open heaven and the Lord's financial blessing is upon me.
- ➤ The devourer has been rebuked for my sake; therefore, my finances will not be wasted.
- ➤ I receive bountifully into my life and bank account, in Jesus' name.
- ➤ God's storehouse is opened upon my life.
- ➤ I am receiving good measure; pressed down, shaken together, and running over shall men give unto me, in Jesus' name.
- ➤ I am reaping from all the seeds I have sown into the kingdom of God, in Jesus' name.
- ➤ The wealth of the unjust is laid up for me, in Jesus' name.
- ➤ God is supplying all my needs according to His riches in glory, in Jesus' name.
- ➤ All generations are calling me blessed.
- ➤ Gold and silver belongs to God, and all that the Father has is mine, in Jesus' name.
- ➤ I will never see lack in my life, in Jesus' name.
- ➤ As I give to the poor, I am lending to the Lord. Whenever I am in need of money, the Lord will supply.

- All grace is abounding toward me. I have sufficiency in all things.
- I operate in abundance.
- I am blessed in gold, silver, and riches.
- Financial doors are being opened unto me, in Jesus' name.
- I pay my tithes, therefore my name is written in the book of remembrance, in Jesus' name.
- The blessing of God is upon me, therefore I will never be a candidate for bad investment.
- My money will never be wasted.
- Whenever I am in need of money, my God will make a way where there is no way.
- I am free from financial bondage.
- God has enlarged my borders and enlarged my coast.
- The Lord is giving me ideas for financial advancement.
- The Lord has blessed me with money-making ideas, in Jesus' name.

Begin to thank the Lord in Jesus' name for financial breakthroughs.

Chapter 3

BLESSINGS ON YOUR BODY

Your body is your earth suit; therefore, you need it in order to be here on earth. The moment it deteriorates, you cannot live here anymore. It is very important that you pronounce blessings upon your body always.

Psalm 1:1–3 says,

> Blessed is the man that walketh not in the counsel of the ungodly, nor standeth in the way of sinners, nor sitteth in the seat of the scornful. But his delight is in the law of the Lord; and in his law doth he meditate day and night. And he shall be like a tree planted by the rivers of water, that bringeth forth his fruit in his season; his leaf also

shall not wither; and whatsoever he doeth shall prosper.

Psalm 92:12–14 says,

> The righteous shall flourish like the palm tree: he shall grow like a cedar in Lebanon. Those that be planted in the house of the Lord shall flourish in the courts of our God. They shall still bring forth fruit in old age; they shall be fat and flourishing.

Psalm 128:2 says,

> For thou shalt eat the labour of thine hands: happy shalt thou be, and it shall be well with thee.

Prayer:

➢ The Lord has blessed me with perfect health, in Jesus' name.

➢ I am totally delivered from hair loss, in Jesus' name.

- My eyes are perfect.
- I am blessed with 20/20 vision.
- My optical nerves are working perfectly.
- My arms are very strong.
- I use my hands perfectly.
- All my vital organs are functioning correctly, by divine movements.
- My skeletal structure is in order.
- My feet are strong.
- My skin is bright and healthy.
- My body is in perfect shape.
- I am blessed with a strong body, even in my old age; the Lord will still preserve my body to function perfectly.
- My whole body is blessed.
- My reproductive organs are functioning well.
- My jaws function well, my teeth are strong.
- All infirmities have been lifted off my body in Jesus' name, and I am well.

Chapter 4

BLESSINGS ON YOUR CLOTHING

My reason for blessing clothing is something the Lord laid on my heart a long time ago. In times past, mothers made clothing for their children and the rest of the family. Now, times have changed; people buy clothing from shops, yet wonder why children are suffering from all kinds of diseases. Most manufacturers and designers are not godly, and they will go to any lengths in the occult to sell their products. Many enact numerous rituals before releasing their products for sale. This affects not only children's clothing, but all clothing, accessories—everything that we wear. This is the reason we have to bless the things we wear.

When you buy and bring home new clothes, the first thing to do is to bless them. Often, they are tried on by many people at the shop before you buy them. Isn't it appropriate, then, to bless them before you wear them?

Acts 19:11–12 says,

> And God wrought special miracles by the hands of Paul: So that from his body were brought unto the sick handkerchiefs or aprons, and the diseases departed from them, and the evil spirits went out of them.

In the same way that an anointed man's clothing brings healing and blessing, evil people's clothing will bring whatever they represent to you. Remember that the woman with the issue of blood touched the hem of Jesus' garment and was made whole.

PRAYER:

- ➢ Father, remove every contamination from my clothing and shoes.
- ➢ Father, bless my clothing in the name of Jesus.

- Bless my shirts, dresses, trousers/pants, and underwear.
- Bless my hats, caps, scarves, eyeglasses, earmuffs, head scarves, and hair accessories.
- Bless my sleepwear.
- Bless my shoes, boots, and bedroom slippers.
- Bless my jewelry: my earrings, necklaces, bracelets, chains, and beads.
- Lord, bless everything I wear on my body, in Jesus' name.

Chapter 5

BLESSINGS ON YOUR BUSINESS

Deuteronomy 15:10–11 says,

> Thou shalt surely give him, and thine heart
> shall not be grieved when thou givest unto
> him: because that for this thing the Lord
> thy God shall bless thee in all thy works,
> and in all that thou puttest thine hand
> unto. For the poor shall never cease out
> of the land: therefore I command thee,
> saying, Thou shalt open thine hand wide
> unto thy brother, to thy poor, and to thy
> needy, in thy land.

The Lord will bless your business when you are kind to the poor.

2 Corinthians 9:8 says,

> And God is able to make all grace abound toward you; that ye, always having all sufficiency in all things, may abound to every good work.

Many Christians want God to bless them, but they do not want to give. It does not work like that; there is a principle.

Prayer:

- ➢ Father, in the name of Jesus, bless my business.
- ➢ Bless the land on which my business stands.
- ➢ Give me faithful customers.
- ➢ Bring faithful clients and connect my business with them.
- ➢ Bless my business and help me to be a good service provider.

- Bring me good, faithful workers who will not be interested only in their paychecks, but will also render good services in Jesus' name.
- Father, bless my business as I treat my employees well.
- Bless me to see my employees' needs, not just my own.
- When other businesses are folding, do not allow it to affect my business.
- Bless my business with new ideas that will lift it up.
- Help my business to transition whenever it is needed.
- Remove every form of stagnation from my business.
- Bless my business with people who have new ideas to elevate it.
- Bless my business with good lifelong clients and customers.
- Let any person who is a saboteur be far from my business.
- Bless my business as I make You my senior partner.

- ➤ Let my business flourish, and provide it with investors.
- ➤ Let my business expand to have branches in many places.
- ➤ Accelerate my business to the next level.
- ➤ I bless this business not to lay off its workers unnecessarily, in Jesus' name.
- ➤ I bless this business, (*say name of business here*), to be a blessing to its employees.

Chapter 6

BLESSINGS ON YOUR PLACE OF WORK

Psalm 91:1-16. The year 2001 we saw the incident known in the United States as 9/11. It was a catastrophe that will always be noted in history as one of the most diabolical operations of the wickedness of man. This was the bombing by terrorists of the World Trade Center in New York City. Many people died and many others were injured, all by the wickedness of man.

Nobody knows what will happen in the next hour at your job. Many people have been delivered from harm through God's intervention. I heard through my sister one lady's testimony: she said that she always kissed and bid her young child good-bye before she left for work. On this particular day, her child kept shying away from her. She kept calling and running after the child to say good-bye. This caused her to miss her usual train. When she got to her workplace, she saw that the building was on fire. She had escaped catastrophe. Her office was in the twin towers of the World Trade Center.

God divinely delivered some people from the World Trade Centre bombing on 9/11. Some people went out to buy something, and that delivered them from that disaster; others just walked into it and died. This is why it is important that we bless our workplace.

Prayer:

- ➢ Father, bless my place of work, (*say name of workplace here*).
- ➢ I bless my place of work in Jesus name.
- ➢ Let the protective hand of God be upon my place of work, in Jesus' name.
- ➢ Let all the people at my workplace be blessed, in Jesus' name.
- ➢ Lord, surround my workplace with your protective angels, in Jesus' name.

- ➢ Lord, protect me, my boss, and my coworkers, in Jesus' name.
- ➢ Let our place of work be blessed, and keep our environment safe, in Jesus' name.
- ➢ Let there never be any disaster in my workplace, in Jesus' name.
- ➢ Let the business be successful so all the workers will feel safe to produce their best, in Jesus' name.
- ➢ Let there be peace among the workers, in Jesus' name.
- ➢ I bless and cast out groupings and divisions, by the power of the Holy Spirit, in Jesus' name.

Chapter 7

BLESSINGS ON YOUR SONS

Psalm 128:1–6 says,

> Blessed is every one that feareth the Lord;
> that walketh in his ways. For thou shalt
> eat the labour of thine hands: happy shalt
> thou be, and it shall be well with thee.
> Thy wife shall be as a fruitful vine by the
> sides of thine house: thy children like olive
> plants round about thy table. Behold, that
> thus shall the man be blessed that feareth
> the Lord. The Lord shall bless thee out
> of Zion: and thou shalt see the good of
> Jerusalem all the days of thy life. Yea, thou
> shalt see thy children's children, and peace
> upon Israel.

Proverbs 18:22 says,

> Whoso findeth a wife findeth a good thing, and obtaineth favour of the Lord.

Proverbs 20:7 says,

> The just man walketh in his integrity: his children are blessed after him.

Prayer:

- ➢ The Lord bless you as you fear Him.
- ➢ You will eat the labor of your hand.
- ➢ The Lord bless you with a good, loving wife.
- ➢ Your wife will be like a fruitful vine by the side of your house.
- ➢ Your children will be blessed like olive plants round about your table.
- ➢ You will live to see your children's children.
- ➢ You will be a blessed man.
- ➢ Your land will be blessed.
- ➢ The Lord will bless the work of your hands.
- ➢ You will operate in perfect health.

- Your children will be respectful and they will respect you just as you love their mother.
- Your home will be peaceful.
- You will be blessed with a loving home.
- You will be blessed above your fellows.
- Whatsoever you set your face to do, you will be blessed in it.
- You will be blessed when you go out, and when you come in.
- You will repel evil friends and evil people.
- You will attract good people.
- Any person whom you are not supposed to meet—you will not meet them.
- You will meet those whom you are supposed to meet.
- You will never fall prey to circumstances.
- You will have favor with God, and favor with men, in Jesus' name.
- You will serve God all the days of your life.
- You are a God-fearing man.
- You will cheat no one and no one will cheat you.
- The Lord bless you and enlarge your coast and your borders.
- Where ever you go, you will be blessed.

- You will have financial acumen.
- Poverty will be far from you.
- May the Lord give you good friends who will influence you positively.
- Be a good son to your father and mother.
- Be a good brother to your siblings.
- May you be a strong man, physically, emotionally, psychologically, and economically, in Jesus' name.
- Be a good husband to your wife.
- Be a good father to your children.
- May you live long to accomplish your purpose in Jesus' name.
- May the Lord give you wisdom and understanding. May the Lord give you strength all the days of your life.
- Let your fountain be blessed, and rejoice with the wife of thy youth (Proverbs 5:18).

Chapter 8

BLESSINGS ON YOUR DAUGHTERS

Proverbs 19:14 says,

> House and riches are the inheritance of
> fathers: and a prudent wife is from the Lord.

Please read Proverbs 31:10–31 and Job 40.

Prayer:

- ➤ The Lord bless you with perfect health.
- ➤ May you be strong all the days of your life.
- ➤ May the Lord Jehovah be your guide always.
- ➤ May you be a blessing to your father and mother.

- ➤ May you be a blessing to your siblings.
- ➤ May you be blessed to make right choices in life.
- ➤ May you be a good, virtuous woman to yourself, your husband, and your children.
- ➤ May you be a wise counselor to your husband and your children.
- ➤ May you be a great helpmate to your husband.
- ➤ May you be fruitful and have many children.
- ➤ May your words be gracious whenever you open your mouth.
- ➤ May you never be a victim of any man.
- ➤ May God give you a good, loving, and understanding husband who will love and cherish you all the days of your life.
- ➤ May your home be the home of a virtuous woman, as in Proverbs 31:10–31.
- ➤ May God bless you with good children.
- ➤ May your body be strong, even in your old age.
- ➤ May you never be named among the evil.
- ➤ May God supply all your needs.
- ➤ May your heart be filled with kindness and love for others.
- ➤ May you respect your husband and his family.

➢ May blessing abound toward you all the days of your life.

➢ May you never see lack in your life.

➢ May the Lord prosper you to fulfill your destiny in life, in Jesus' name.

➢ Your latter shall be greater than your former, in Jesus' name.

Chapter 9

BLESSINGS ON YOUR YOUNG CHILDREN (BABIES, TODDLERS, TEENS)

The best time to begin to pronounce blessing on children is before, or at the time that you become pregnant, although it is never too late to pronounce blessing, at any age.

Luke 1:41 says,

> And It came to pass, that, when Elisabeth heard the salutation of Mary, the babe leaped in her womb; and Elisabeth was filled with the Holy Ghost.

Babies in the womb hear and sense blessing. They sense danger as well. Begin to bless them while they are in the womb. As you pronounce these blessings on them, see God establishing all that you say in their lives.

Genesis 25:26 says,

> And after that came his brother out, and his hand took hold on Esau's heel; and his name was called Jacob: and Isaac was threescore years old when she bare them.

The Bible says that Jacob and Esau were struggling in their mother's womb. They were two nations, two different and unfriendly nations sharing the same womb. That's why blessings must be implemented, and pronounced vigorously on children when they are in the womb; this way, they become friendly nations with each other in the case of twins, or multiple pregnancies.

Prayer:

➤ May you be blessed with a good and honest heart.

- May you be a blessed baby.
- May you find favor with God, and favor with men, all the days of your life.
- May God prepare good friends for you while you are growing up.
- May you have a good temperament.
- May all your virtues be preserved unto you.
- May no one steal any of your virtues or benefits.
- May the Lord protect your school, and all the schools you attend.
- May you never be a victim of circumstance.
- May your friends be good friends that never lead you into problems and disaster.
- May you be a healthy child.
- May you have a blessed childhood.
- May disaster never find you anywhere.
- May you grow in the fear of God and love His word.
- May you be guarded by the word of God to make right choices in life.
- May you never meet anyone who will lead you astray.
- May you never be enticed to do evil to anyone, all the days of your life.

- ➤ May you learn to choose good over evil.
- ➤ May the word of God guide you.
- ➤ May you be the head and not the tail.
- ➤ May evil never find you.
- ➤ May you have sharp brains for studying.
- ➤ May you be an excellent student.
- ➤ May God give you great ideas to help your generation.
- ➤ May you be a blessing to your generation all the days of your life.
- ➤ May you be a good friend.
- ➤ May you be a caring person to your siblings, friends, father, mother, teachers, and all who cross your path.
- ➤ May you never be in the wrong place at the wrong time.
- ➤ May you never meet anyone who will lead you into disaster.
- ➤ May your environment be blessed.
- ➤ May you be a blessing to your father and mother, in Jesus' name.
- ➤ You will excel in whatever you do; you will prove to be excellent in all you do.

- I declare that you shall walk in the fullness of your destiny.
- May you be the best in the unique thing that God created you for.
- May the Lord grant unto you divine acceleration.
- May the Lord grant unto you strength, excellence, dignity, and power in the Lord.
- Be honorable in this life.
- You will live to be the number of years that God gave you.
- There will be no untimely death in your life.
- You will be mighty on the face of the earth, in Jesus name.

Chapter 10

BLESSINGS ON YOUR LAND

In Genesis 3:17–19, the Lord pronounced a very harsh curse on the ground because of Adam's disobedience. He ate of the Tree of Knowledge of Good and Evil when God had specifically instructed him not to, so the ground became cursed. God always has an antidote for curses like that.

2 Chronicles 7:14 says,

> If my people, which are called by my name, shall humble themselves, and pray, and seek my face, and turn from their wicked ways; then will I hear from heaven, and will forgive their sin, and will heal their land.

Most lands carry curses due to ancestral idolatry and evil sacrifices. Therefore, it is necessary that land be blessed by its occupants. Even if the land has been in your family for years, it is very important for you, as the present occupant, to pronounce blessings upon it. This way, your land will not be one that devours its inhabitants. First, break all curses on the land before you pronounce the blessing. For example, say, "Father, I ask for forgiveness for every sacrilegious operation that has occurred on this land. I break every curse on this land in the name of Jesus."

Prayer:

> ➢ I bless this land in the name of Jesus.
> ➢ This land is a land flowing with milk and honey.
> ➢ All the people who occupy this land will be blessed.
> ➢ Everything that is planted on this land will yield its increase.
> ➢ All the trees on this land will grow to the maximum.

- ➤ Every vegetable that is planted on this land will grow larger than its normal size.
- ➤ Every herb that is planted on this land will be very potent.
- ➤ All flowers that are planted on this land will bud with the most beautiful flowers.
- ➤ Everybody who lives on this land will live long.
- ➤ The wells dug on this land will produce healthy water.
- ➤ The lawn on this land will be very healthy and green.
- ➤ There will be no termites or any evil insects or pests on this land.
- ➤ Over all, this land is a blessed land.
- ➤ There will be no flooding of this land or the properties on it.
- ➤ The ground of this land will swallow any water that would cause flooding in this place.
- ➤ Every property on this land will have divine protection.
- ➤ Children born on this land will excel, in Jesus' name.
- ➤ The waters will be within their own province, in Jesus' name.

Chapter 11

BLESSINGS ON YOUR FAMILY (BY THE FATHER)

Prayer:

> ➤ Lord, bless my wife and give her a kind heart toward me.

> ➤ Bless me with a good home.

> ➤ Let my family be a God-fearing family.

> ➤ Holy Spirit, help us to put God first in all we do.

> ➤ Give us a desire to serve God and put the things of God first in our lives.

> ➤ Bless us financially so that we may give for the advancement of the work of God, in Jesus' name.

- ➤ Whatever we do, let us acknowledge God and honor God in our decision making.
- ➤ Let us fear God in our home.
- ➤ Lord, bless us with children who will serve You.
- ➤ Direct us to a good home church where we will grow spiritually.
- ➤ Bless our home and grant my family financial independence.
- ➤ Lead us into making good financial investments.
- ➤ Bless us, O God, with good health.
- ➤ Lord, bless my wife with good health.
- ➤ Bless me with good health.
- ➤ Bless us with healthy children, in Jesus' name.
- ➤ Bless our neighborhood; let our neighborhood be safe, in Jesus' name.
- ➤ Bless my family to be lenders, not borrowers, in Jesus' name.

Chapter 12

BLESSINGS ON YOUR FAMILY (BY THE MOTHER)

Proverbs 31:25–30 says,

> Strength and honour are her clothing; and she shall rejoice in time to come. She openeth her mouth with wisdom; and in her tongue is the law of kindness. She looketh well to the ways of her household, and eateth not the bread of idleness. Her children arise up, and call her blessed; her husband also, and he praiseth her. Many daughters have done virtuously, but thou excellest them all. Favour is deceitful, and beauty is vain: but a woman that feareth the Lord, she shall be praised.

A woman as wife and mother in the home is a great blessing. The Bible says she opens her mouth with wisdom. Many things affect the woman in the home; caring for children and the husband can be so challenging sometimes. Sometimes, when a woman is under pressure, the words that come out of her mouth may not be that gracious. But beginning to practice blessing your household will start to change things around you.

This is especially true when a husband is not the loving man you expect him to be. Let your words be gracious, seasoned with salt. Change your environment with the pronouncement of blessing upon your entire household.

Prayer:

> - Father, bless my husband and grant him a heart of flesh and remove the heart of stone from him.
> - Bless our household with joy unspeakable.
> - Bless me with a kind heart to love my family, my husband, and my children.
> - Father, bless my husband with a good job.
> - Bless my husband's business; let it flourish.

- Bless our household with love and understanding.
- Bless us with good health.
- Father, bless my husband with long life so we can be together longer than the average couple.
- Bless us with godly children.
- Father, bless our children to make headway in life.
- Let all our children excel in their callings, in Jesus' name.
- Bless our neighborhood.
- Bless our environment, in Jesus' name.
- Father, give me a heart to love my husband's family, in Jesus' name.

Chapter 13

BLESSINGS FOR YOUR GRANDSON

If you are blessing him in his presence, say these blessings in the second person. For example: "May God give *you* a good wife."

Prayer:

- ➤ Father, today I bless my grandson, (*say name here*), in the name of Jesus.
- ➤ Let the blessing of God overtake and overshadow him, in Jesus' name.
- ➤ Fill his heart with the fear of God.
- ➤ Give him a good, godly wife, a virtuous woman as described in Proverbs 31.

- ➢ Father, help him to live to see his own grandchildren and great-grandchildren.
- ➢ Father, bless (*say name here*) with good, God-fearing children.
- ➢ Help him to train his children in the fear of God.
- ➢ Father, bless his home; let his home be a place of joy.
- ➢ Let him be a good husband and a good father to his wife and children.
- ➢ May God anoint him to be a great captain of his ship.
- ➢ May God bless him to be a great man who will affects his generation.
- ➢ May God grant him all his heart's desire.
- ➢ May he never depart from the precepts and ordinances of God.
- ➢ May he never be a victim of circumstance.
- ➢ May the Lord deliver him from all evil and all appearances of evil.
- ➢ May he live to be an honest man.
- ➢ May he leave a great legacy to his children and his children's children.

Chapter 14

BLESSINGS ON YOUR GRANDDAUGHTER

Prayer:

- ➢ Father, today I bless my granddaughter, (*say name here*), in the name of Jesus.
- ➢ May God bless you and keep you; let His face shine upon you.
- ➢ May you excel in all your endeavors, in Jesus' name.
- ➢ May you live to see your children's children.
- ➢ May God give you a good, loving, and understanding husband.
- ➢ May you live to be a virtuous woman as described in Proverbs 31.

- ➤ Be a good wife to your husband and a good mother to your children.
- ➤ May God give you good friends.
- ➤ May you never be in the wrong place at the wrong time.
- ➤ May goodness and mercy follow you all the days of your life.
- ➤ May you live to affect your generation.
- ➤ May you have perfect health and long life, in Jesus' name.

Chapter 15

BLESSINGS ON YOUR BROTHER

Prayer:

- ➤ Father, bless my brother, (*say name here*).
- ➤ Father, bless him to make the right choices in life.
- ➤ Father, bless him with a good life. Let him never have any problems with the law of the land, in Jesus' name.
- ➤ Bless (*say name here*) financially.
- ➤ Bless him with a good wife.
- ➤ Bless my brother's wife to be the best spouse.
- ➤ Let her be a blessing to my brother.
- ➤ Bless my brother to have good and healthy children.

- ➢ Bless my brother with perfect health.
- ➢ Bless my brother's work/business. Let him be the head and not the tail.
- ➢ Give my brother good friends, not ones that will lead him into trouble.
- ➢ Lord bless my brother with long life and prosper his ways.
- ➢ Let my brother have a peaceful home, in Jesus' name.

Chapter 16

BLESSINGS ON YOUR SISTER

Prayer:

- ➤ Father, bless my sister, (*say name here*).
- ➤ Bless (*say name here*) to make the right choices in life.
- ➤ Lord, bless my sister with perfect health.
- ➤ Bless my sister and her family (*if she is married*).
- ➤ Bless my sister with a perfect marriage.
- ➤ Bless my sister to find a good husband (*if she is not married*).
- ➤ Lord, bless her with a man who will love her for who she is.
- ➤ Give my sister a good job.
- ➤ Bless my sister's business to yield dividends, in Jesus' name.

- ➤ Bless my sister to have favor with God and with men.
- ➤ Father, bless my sister with good friends.
- ➤ Bless my sister to choose to be a virtuous woman as described in Proverbs 31:10–31.
- ➤ Father, bless my sister with a good heart to be a blessing to me, to her husband, and to her children.
- ➤ Bless my sister to serve you well, in Jesus' name.

Chapter 17

BLESSINGS ON YOUR UNCLE

Prayer:

- ➤ Father, bless my uncle, (*say name here*).
- ➤ Bless my uncle's family, his wife, and his children.
- ➤ Father, bless my uncle with perfect health.
- ➤ Bless my uncle's home with peace.
- ➤ Bless my uncle's business.
- ➤ Bless my uncle on his job.
- ➤ Father, protect my uncle all the days of his life.
- ➤ Father, bless my uncle with the fear of the Lord.
- ➤ Father, let my uncle serve You and serve You well, in Jesus' name.

Chapter 18

BLESSINGS ON YOUR AUNT

Prayer:

- ➢ Father, bless my aunt, (*say name here*).
- ➢ Bless my aunt's home; give her peace and love in her home.
- ➢ Father, bless my aunt with excellent health.
- ➢ Father, let my aunt live long.
- ➢ Bless my aunt's business.
- ➢ Bless my aunt on her job.
- ➢ Bless everything my aunt sets her face to do.

Chapter 19

BLESSINGS ON YOUR NEPHEW

Prayer:

- ➤ Father, bless my nephew (*say name here*). (*If you have more than one nephew, mention their names one by one and bless each of them.*)
- ➤ Bless my nephew to excel in his education.
- ➤ Bless my nephew with good health.
- ➤ Father, bless my nephew with good friends.
- ➤ Deliver my nephew from making bad friends.
- ➤ Bless my nephew never to encounter problems with the law.
- ➤ Bless my nephew with long life, in Jesus' name.
- ➤ Bless my nephew with talents that will affect his generation.

➢ When the time is due, Lord, give my nephew a good wife.

➢ Bless him with good children.

➢ Bless my nephew with a good life.

➢ Father, let (say name here) fear You and serve You well, in Jesus' name.

Chapter 20

BLESSINGS ON YOUR NIECE

Prayer:

- ➤ Father, bless my niece, (*say name here*).
- ➤ Bless my niece with peace of mind to concentrate on her studies.
- ➤ Bless my niece with good friends.
- ➤ Bless my niece to excel in all she does.
- ➤ Bless my niece with a good husband when the time is due.
- ➤ Lord, fill her heart with the fear of God.
- ➤ Let her be a good wife to her husband.
- ➤ Bless her with perfect health.
- ➤ Father, let (say name here) be successful in all she does, in Jesus' name.

Chapter 21

BLESSINGS ON YOUR CHILDREN'S SCHOOL

Not too long ago, the Columbine High School massacre took place. On April 20th, 1999, two seniors, Eric Harris and Dylan Klebold, opened fire on their school, injuring twenty-one students and murdering twelve students and one teacher. Three others were injured as they attempted to escape the school. The pair then committed suicide.

In 1999 alone, there were six recorded school shootings in the United States. There are probably also numerous attacks that we don't get to hear about in the news.

The most heart-wrenching shooting in recent time occurred at Sandy Hook Elementary School in Newton, Connecticut, on December 14, 2012. Twenty-year-old

Adam Lanza fatally shot and killed twenty children and six adults. He also killed his mother and himself.

Christians are the preservers of the earth. We have to bless the schools our children attend. We can also bless the other schools around the area.

Prayer:

- ➢ Father, bless my child's school, in Jesus' name.
- ➢ Bless all the children who attend the school.
- ➢ Let there be peace in the school.
- ➢ Father, I ask You to deliver all the children in the school from any mental anguish that would cause them to become a problem to any other child.
- ➢ Lord, surround the school with Your angels to protect my child, all the children, and all their teachers.
- ➢ Father, heal all the children in the school who have emotional problems.
- ➢ Lord, quickly expose any problems of students or workers at the school before they turn into a diabolical situation, in Jesus' name.

Chapter 22

BLESSINGS ON YOUR CHILDREN'S TEACHERS

Prayer:

- ➢ Father, let the board have godly teachers for the kids at this school.
- ➢ Lord, give the teachers good hearts to impart knowledge to the children in their classes.
- ➢ Father, bless all the teachers in the school.
- ➢ Give the teachers happy homes so they will not transfer their problems from home to school.
- ➢ Bless the teachers' families and their children.
- ➢ Bless the teachers with honest hearts.
- ➢ Deliver all the teachers from every form of prejudice.
- ➢ Let the teachers be godly teachers, in Jesus' name.

Chapter 23

BLESSINGS ON YOUR MALE CHILD'S FRIENDS

There are numerous reasons you should bless your children's friends. They may influence your children positively or negatively.

Proverbs 22:24–25 says,

> Make no friendship with an angry man;
> and with a furious man thou shalt not go:
> Lest thou learn his ways, and get a snare
> to thy soul.

Proverbs 27:17 says,

Iron sharpeneth iron; so a man sharpeneth
the countenance of his friend.

Everybody needs a good friend. It is good to pray for God to give your children good friends, and when they find them, bless them as you bless your own children. James 4:4 declares that friendship with the world is enmity with God.

When you pray for godly friends for your child, God will bring them.

Prayer:

> Father, in the name of Jesus, bless my child's friend, (*say name here*).
> Protect and deliver him from trouble.
> Help him to never fall victim to circumstance.
> Bless his young life, let him achieve his purpose.
> Bless him make good choices in life.
> Bless his parents with the wisdom to train him very well.
> Bless him with talents and gifts to affect his generation positively.

- Bless him with a good life partner, a virtuous wife, in Jesus' name.
- Bless him to take his education seriously.
- Bless him with perfect health.
- Let him not be a snare to my son, in Jesus' name.
- Bless him to affect my son positively.
- Bless him and let his dreams come true.
- Bless him with the fear of the Lord.
- Make him successful in all his endeavors.

Chapter 24

BLESSINGS ON YOUR FEMALE CHILD'S FRIENDS

Prayer:

- ➢ Father, in the name of Jesus, bless my child's friend, (*say name here*).
- ➢ Bless her with perfect health, in Jesus' name.
- ➢ Bless her live to be the number of years You have given her.
- ➢ Help her to make the right choices in life.
- ➢ Father, always protect her from evil people, in the name of Jesus.
- ➢ Bless her with gifts and talents to affect her generation.
- ➢ Let her be a good friend to my child and affect my child positively.

> Give her a heart to serve You.
> Father, when the time is due, give her a good, loving, and understanding husband.
> Let her be a good wife and a good mother.
> Help her to achieve her purpose in this life.

Chapter 25

BLESSINGS ON YOUR WIFE'S FRIENDS

Prayer:

- ➤ Father, bless my wife's friend. (*You can mention a specific name if you want.*)
- ➤ Help her to make all the right choices in this life.
- ➤ Let her be a blessing to her husband and her children.
- ➤ Bless her business or job, in Jesus' name.
- ➤ Let her life be a blessing for her generation.
- ➤ Let every influence that she has to offer my wife be a positive one.
- ➤ Father, bless her family.
- ➤ Bless her to be a blessing to us, in Jesus' name.

Chapter 26

BLESSINGS ON YOUR HUSBAND'S FRIENDS

Prayer:

> ➤ Father, bless my husband's friend. (*You can mention a specific name if you want.*)
> ➤ Father, bless him make the right choices in life.
> ➤ Father, bless him with a positive attitude toward my husband.
> ➤ Let there not be any kind of jealousy in his heart toward my husband.
> ➤ Bless his wife and children.
> ➤ Bless him make the right choice in choosing a good wife that will be a blessing to him and to us.
> ➤ Bless him with good children.

- ➢ Bless his business and make it a successful one.
- ➢ Bless him with perfect health, in Jesus' name.
- ➢ Father, bless him with the fear of God.

Chapter 27

BLESSINGS ON YOUR NEIGHBOR

Your neighbors are very important in your life.

Proverbs 27:10 says,

> Thine own friend, and thy father's friend,
> forsake not; neither go into thy brother's
> house in the day of thy calamity: for better
> is a neighbor that is near than a brother
> far off.

That is why it is so important that you treat your neighbors well. For example, if something happens to you, your neighbor is the next person you would call for assistance. You will call your neighbor before calling family members who live a distance away.

In Matthew 22:39, Jesus said,

> And the second is like unto it, Thou shalt love thy neighbor as thyself.

It is very important that you bless your neighbors.

Prayer:

- ➤ Father, bless my neighbors, (say names here).
- ➤ Bless their children, (*say names here*).
- ➤ Father, bless them with perfect health.
- ➤ Let them excel in all they do.
- ➤ Let them serve You well.
- ➤ Bless the work of their hands.
- ➤ Bless them with long life.
- ➤ Give them peace in their home, in Jesus' name.

Chapter 28

BLESSINGS ON YOUR BOSS

Genesis 30:27 declares,

> And Laban said unto him, I pray thee, if I
> have found favour in thine eyes, tarry: for
> I have learned by experience that the Lord
> hath blessed me for thy sake.

But when God, started blessing Jacob there arose jealousy
against Jacob. And Laban's children started complaining.

Genesis 30:43 says,

> And the man increased exceedingly, and
> had much cattle, and maidservants, and
> menservants, and camels, and asses.

Genesis 31:1–2 declares,

> And he heard the words of Laban's sons, saying, Jacob hath taken away all that was our father's; and of that which was our father's hath he gotten all this glory. And Jacob beheld the countenance of Laban, and, behold, it was not toward him as before.

When you read the whole of chapter 31, you can see that the spirit of jealousy had engulfed Laban and his sons against Jacob.

Verse 9 says,

> Thus God hath taken away the cattle of your father, and given them to me.

God can cause you to prosper above your boss; this, in turn, can create havoc and confusion in your work place—that is, if your boss does not have the mind of Christ. If your boss does not know Christ, pray for his or her conversion, but don't jump on him or her with your opinions. Just privately pray for the Lord to open a way for him or her to be saved.

You must bless your boss so that if he decides to hurt you, the Lord will defend you, or so that the Lord will give you favor before your boss.

Prayer:

- ➤ Father, bless my boss, (*say name here*), in Jesus' name.
- ➤ Let him/her be blessed in every area of his/her life.
- ➤ Bless his/her spouse, in Jesus' name.
- ➤ Give my boss and his/her family good health.
- ➤ Bless his/her children in the name of Jesus.
- ➤ Whatever my boss, (*say name here*), does, let him/her prosper in it.
- ➤ Let his/her business flourish and expand, in Jesus' name.
- ➤ Bless my boss financially.
- ➤ Father, give my boss a peaceful home so that his/her workers will not suffer because of his/her problems at home.

➢ Bless my boss to have a kind heart for his/her employees.

➢ Give my boss peace of mind to relate to his/her workers in a positive way.

➢ Let there always be a cordial relationship between my boss and me.

➢ Bless my boss with the peace of mind so he/she can be the best boss ever.

Chapter 29

BLESSINGS ON YOUR ASSOCIATES AND COWORKERS

Prayer:

➤ Father, bless my associates and coworkers, in Jesus' name.

➤ Bless them to work harmoniously so that there will be no friction on the job.

➤ Let every one of my associates produce their best on the job.

➤ Let each and every one of my associates have good intentions for the business.

➤ Father, make each one of them an asset, not a liability.

➤ Father, prosper each of my associates and coworkers, in Jesus' name.

Chapter 30

BLESSINGS ON
YOUR FRIENDS

Prayer:

- ➤ Father, bless my friend. (*You can mention a specific name if you want.*)
- ➤ Help him/her to be successful in life.
- ➤ Bless him/her with the ability to serve You well.
- ➤ Fill him/her with the Holy Spirit to make the right choices, in Jesus' name.
- ➤ Let him/her be able to succeed in his/her choice of profession.
- ➤ Bless his/her family and bless him/her to make the right choice in choosing the right life partner, in Jesus' name.
- ➤ Bless him/her with long life and prosper his/her ways. Give him/her perfect health, in Jesus' name.

Chapter 31

BLESSINGS ON YOUR FAMILY FRIENDS

Prayer:

- ➤ Father, bless the *(say family name of friends here, for example, "The Taylors").*
- ➤ Let there be peace in their family.
- ➤ Bless them individually.
- ➤ Bless them with long lives and give them physical health.
- ➤ Bless them financially.
- ➤ Help them to always make the right choices.
- ➤ Bless their endeavors, in Jesus' name.

Chapter 32

BLESSINGS ON YOUR ENEMIES

Sometimes we are reluctant to bless people who have harassed us, or persecuted us in some way, but the Lord admonishes us in the book of Matthew to love our enemies. It is very strange for an unbeliever to understand this, but the Lord Jesus Christ is all wisdom. He wants us to be different from the rest of the world.

Matthew 5:44–45 says,

> But I say unto you, Love your enemies, bless them that curse you, do good to them that hate you, and pray for them which despitefully use you, and persecute you; That ye may be the children of your Father

which is in heaven: for he maketh his sun to rise on the evil and on the good, and sendeth rain on the just and on the unjust.

Luke 6:27–28 says,

> But I say unto you which hear, Love your enemies, do good to them which hate you, Bless them that curse you, and pray for them which despitefully use you.

When you bless your enemies, you become like Your Lord and Savior. When men spat on Him and beat Him, He prayed for them and said, "Father, forgive them, for they know not what they do."

Proverbs 26:2 says,

> As the bird by wondering, as the swallow by flying, so the curse causeless shall not come."

No curse will settle on you when there is no ground for it.

Proverbs 16:7 says,

> When a man's ways please the Lord, he maketh even his enemies to be at peace with him.

Bless your enemies and see the Lord change situations in your own life. Even your bitterest enemies will be at peace with you. God bless you as you do this!

Prayer:

- ➤ Father, bless my enemies.
- ➤ Bless them to have peace.
- ➤ Let them find You in their hearts.
- ➤ Bless their families.
- ➤ Father, give them perfect health.
- ➤ Bless them to make the right choices in this life.
- ➤ Let their hearts' desires come true.

- ➤ Bless them to drop every opposition against me, or any person that they have bitterness against in their hearts.
- ➤ Fill their hearts with a desire to know and serve You, Lord.
- ➤ Fill their hearts with love for others.
- ➤ Help them to do this, in Jesus' name.

Chapter 33

BLESSINGS ON YOUR ENVIRONMENT

➤ Father, bless our neighborhood.

➤ Bless the businesses in my neighborhood, in Jesus' name.

➤ Let the businesses flourish, in Jesus' name.

➤ Father, cancel every environmental terror, in Jesus' name.

➤ Let the people who live in this area be blessed.

➤ Let the people who live in this area serve You, Lord.

➤ Remove every plantation of evil from this area, in Jesus' name.

➤ Father, let the grounds be blessed.

➤ Let the people in this area have good children.

- ➤ Father, turn every curse in this area into blessing, in Jesus' name.
- ➤ Father, remove any termite problem from this area.
- ➤ Lord, deliver the land from pests and every environmental disaster, in Jesus' name.
- ➤ Bless this area and remove any flood problem from this area.
- ➤ I speak to (*say name of nearby sea, river, creek, etc. here*): in the name of Jesus, stay within your province.
- ➤ I challenge every evil weed not to grow in this area anymore, in Jesus' name.
- ➤ Father, let every evil tree in this area wither and die, in Jesus' name.
- ➤ Father, let every evil animal in this area go very far from this neighborhood, in Jesus' name.
- ➤ Father, bless this area and do not allow any evil to flourish here, in Jesus' name.

Chapter 34

BLESSINGS FOR THE ENLARGEMENT OF YOUR COAST

Prayer:

- ➤ I pray that Thou wouldest enlarge my coast.
- ➤ Let Your hand be with me.
- ➤ Keep me from evil, O Lord, that it would not grieve me.
- ➤ God, bless me and grant me my request.

Chapter 35

BLESSINGS ON LOCAL BUSINESSES

Blessing the businesses in your area is very important. My family once lived in a neighborhood that used to have many businesses. When one store caught fire, it affected three other businesses. One grocery store that was a walking distance from our apartment building closed down, and it affected a fish shop in the neighborhood which closed down too. I realized that everything in the area was going down. We had to travel to another area to buy food from the grocery store there. When the owners of that grocery store realized there was a high volume of people coming to their shop, they hiked up their prices. They realized that, the customers had no choice but to pay whatever they were charging.

That was when the Lord laid on my heart to start praying for my neighborhood businesses. As I did, the former grocery building was bought by Pioneer Food chain store, which opened a new grocery store on the same premises. The businesses around the area started excelling. The store that got burnt down had been a big pharmacy; it was reopened with a gift shop attached to it. I could see that when we pray for our local businesses, God hears us.

Prayer:

- ➤ Father, I pray and bless the businesses around this area, in Jesus' name. (*You can go around the neighborhood and list the names of the businesses in the area.*)
- ➤ Let all the businesses in this area be blessed with good workers, in Jesus' name.
- ➤ Bless the owners of the businesses with kind hearts to take good care of their workers.
- ➤ Let them render good services to their customers.

- ➢ Let anything that will cause problems of fire, disaster, flood, or burglary be stopped, in Jesus' name.
- ➢ Give them divine acceleration, in Jesus' name.
- ➢ Father, let the people in this neighborhood support the businesses here by employing their services and not taking their business elsewhere, in Jesus' name.

Chapter 36

BLESSINGS ON YOUR LAND, PROPERTY, OR ESTATE

The Lord blessed the land before Adam sinned. After the sin of Adam and Eve, the land was cursed. The Bible makes it clear that life and death are in the power of the tongue. It is very important that we open our mouths concerning these things, or, in other words, that we pray.

In Genesis 2:6, the Bible says, "But there went up a mist from the earth, and watered the whole face of the ground." This means that the Lord had placed a mechanism in the earth to recycle itself, but when man sinned, the cycle was reversed.

Genesis 3:17-19 says,

> And unto Adam He said, Because thou
> hast hearkened unto the voice of thy wife,
> and hast eaten of the tree, of which I
> commanded thee, saying, Thou shalt not
> eat of it: cursed is the ground for thy sake;
> in sorrow shalt thou eat of it all the days
> of thy life. Thorns also and thistles shall it
> bring forth to thee; and thou shalt eat the
> herb of the field; In the sweat of thy face
> shalt thou eat bread, till thou return unto
> the ground; for out of it wast thou taken:
> for dust thou art, and unto dust shalt thou
> return.

Those are severe words from God. Although the Bible
says in Galatians 3:13 that "Christ hath redeemed us
from the curse of the law, being made a curse for us: for
it is written, Cursed is every one that hangeth on a tree,"
the land has not been redeemed. We can pronounce the
blessing of God on our land.

2 Chronicles 7:14 says,

> If my people, which are called by my name, shall humble themselves, and pray, and seek my face, and turn from their wicked ways; then will I hear from heaven, and will forgive their sin, and will heal their land.

This simply means that our prayers can change our land completely.

Prayer:

- ➢ Father, bless my land, estate, or property, in Jesus' name.
- ➢ Land, hear the voice of the Lord: yield your increase, in Jesus' name.
- ➢ I bless the land in the name of Jesus.
- ➢ Every thorn and thistle's spirit in this land, in the name of Jesus, hear the voice of the Lord: be gone.
- ➢ Every termite in this land, I command you to die, in Jesus' name.

- ➢ Father, bless this land with minerals to yield its increase, in the name of Jesus.
- ➢ Every power of retardation in this land, be removed, in Jesus' name.
- ➢ Father, let the blessing that you placed in the land before Adam sinned come upon my land, in Jesus' name.
- ➢ Let every tree I plant on this land flourish, in Jesus' name.
- ➢ Father, let every plant I grow on this land flourish, in Jesus' name.
- ➢ Father, let everything I do on this land be a blessing to me, in Jesus' name.
- ➢ Any evil that will come on this land will wither and die, in Jesus' name.
- ➢ Let all the flowers I grow on this land bloom very beautifully, in the name of Jesus.

Chapter 37

BLESSINGS ON
YOUR CHURCH

The church is the body of Christ. The enemy knows this, and it is his most enjoyable agenda to sabotage the church any way he can. The enemy uses people—even pastors, the deacons, the board, or the church members—to bring division and animosity of all kinds to attack Christians and church finances. Attacks can also come from an outside force. Nobody would have thought Judas, one of the disciples of our Lord Jesus Christ who walked with Him for three years, would betray Him.

In Acts 6:1–2, the Bible says,

> And in those days, when the number of
> the disciples was multiplied, there arose

a murmuring of the Grecians against the Hebrews, because their widows were neglected in the daily ministration. Then the twelve called the multitude of the disciples unto them, and said, It is not reason that we should leave the word of God, and serve tables.

When the deacons were chosen, Stephen was among them. He was attacked and killed along with many others. James was killed by Herod, Peter was arrested, and many other obstacles arose in the church. In Corinth, one man slept with his father's wife. First Corinthians 5:1 says, "It is reported commonly that there is fornication among you, and such fornication as is not so much as named among the Gentiles, that one should have his father's wife." These and many problems challenged the church of the Lord daily.

Through the pronouncement of blessings on the church, there will be a transformation on the people and the church as a whole.

Prayer:

- Father, bless our church to be a blessing in our community and the world at large.
- Let the gates of hell be stopped and not prevail in our church, (*say name of church here*).
- Let the presence of God be in our church always.
- Do not let the Spirit of the Lord ever depart from our church.
- Bless our church membership to grow numerically.
- Lord, fill our church with love and understanding.
- Bless our church with people who will help maintain the church building.
- Bless our church with people who will help the pastor, not those who will condemn him or her.
- Let our eyes and our ears be opened, so that when You speak we will hear, and when You reveal, we will understand.
- Bless our church to be able to pay all our bills.
- Bless the church to be able to help our community.
- Father, give us people with a heart for the mission field.

- Bless our church financially to be able to support missions.
- Bless our church with people who will evangelize our neighborhood.
- Bless our church with people with a heart for the poor.
- Bless our church to be a place where those with problems can come and find peace.
- Bless our church members to love each other.
- Bless us with the spirit of unity in our midst.
- Bless our church to be an oasis of love.
- Bless the church to have a heart for the family.
- Bless the individual families in our church.
- Bless the church to have a heart for the single mothers.
- Bless our church, and let all the singles find their own life partners.
- Bless our church to represent You well.
- Let the people fear God. Fill our hearts with the fear of God.
- Bless our children, and let them know you and not be affected by the diabolical things that are going on in this world.
- Bless our church with godly leaders.

- ➤ Remove the spirits of birds and of Jezebel from our church, in Jesus' name.

- ➤ Fill our church with prayerful people who will see need and pray about it.

- ➤ Father, bless our church—especially our pastor and our leaders—with the ability to hear the voice of the Holy Spirit.

- ➤ Bless our pastor to be a great pastor with a heart for You and the poor.

- ➤ Let our pastor be a pastor after Your own heart, in Jesus' name.

- ➤ Bless our church to produce godly leaders.

- ➤ Bless our church to fear God, and our leaders to have a reverential fear of God.

- ➤ Bless our church to represent you well here on earth.

- ➤ Father, let our church be a model of the New Testament church, in the name of Jesus Christ of Nazareth.

- ➤ Bless the universal church of the Lord Jesus Christ.

- ➤ Let our church be a model of the church of Jesus Christ, not the church of man.

- ➤ Bless the church with the gift of the Spirit.

- ➢ Bless the church members to know You and each member to know You experientially.
- ➢ Bless the church members to be faithful to You, Lord.
- ➢ Father, bless the church, and let the members set their priorities right.
- ➢ Bless us and meet our needs.
- ➢ Father, let our church members be like the man in Psalm 1:1–3: "Blessed is the man that walketh not in the counsel of the ungodly, nor standeth in the way of sinners, not sitteth in the seat of the scornful. But his delight is in the law of the Lord; and in his law doth he meditate day and night. And he shall be like a tree planted by the rivers of water, that bringeth forth his fruit in his season; his leaf also shall not wither; and whatsoever he doeth shall prosper."
- ➢ Father, let all those who walk into our church building find Christ and make heaven.
- ➢ Bless us to see and know that we are unique people (1 Peter 2:5–10).

Chapter 38

BLESSINGS ON YOUR PASTOR

If there is anybody we truly have to pray for, it is our own pastor and pastors in general. The work of a pastor is very difficult. I pray that every one of us will take it upon ourselves to pray for them to stay on course.

Acts 20:28–29 declares,

> Take heed therefore unto yourselves, and to all the flock, over the which the Holy Ghost hath made you overseers, to feed the church of God, which he hath purchased with his own blood. For I know this, that after my departing shall grievous wolves enter in among you, not sparing the flock.

Sometimes, when these wolves enter in, if the pastor is not prayerful, then by the time he or she realizes it, the wolves have totally devoured the flock of Jesus Christ.

Jeremiah 3:15 says,

> "And I will give you pastors according to mine heart, which shall feed you with knowledge and understanding."

We need pastors after God's own heart. Pastors must be selfless people who are called by God and are determined to live for Christ, irrespective of what happens. Even if all the people leave a church, the pastor must try not to be discouraged. It is a challenging job, and pastors must learn to encourage themselves, because sometimes, no one else understands them. This is especially important when God has told a pastor to make changes or to take a major decision in the church.

Unfortunately, to be honest, sometimes some of the pastors are the wolves. What do you do when you are faced with such a situation? Pray, Pray, Pray! "Many pastors have destroyed My vineyard, they have trodden my position under foot, they have made my pleasant position a desolate wilderness" (Jeremiah 12:10).

Jeremiah 23:1–2 says,

> Woe be unto the Pastors that destroy and scatter the sheep of my pasture! Saith the Lord. Therefore thus saith the Lord God of Israel against the Pastors that feed my people; Ye have scattered my flock, and driven them away, and have not visited them: behold, I will visit upon you the evil of your doings, saith the Lord.

Let us bless them and God will do the rest. Pastors are a gift to the church, and we have to respect them and bless them at all times, knowing that, while some have just crept in, others are really called by God. God is the judge, not us. He will build His church and the gates of hell shall not prevail against it.

Prayer:

➢ Father, bless our pastor in the name of Jesus.

- Father, let him/her be the man/woman of God You called him/her to be.
- Father, bless our pastor to be strong in You.
- Let him/her take his/her work very seriously and make his/her calling sure.
- Let him/her seek you day and night.
- Let our pastor hear from You.
- Open his/her eyes and open his/her ears so that when You reveal, he/she will see, and when You speak, he/she will hear.
- Father, bless him/her with the heart of a shepherd.
- Bless him/her with a mind to know whose he/she is, in the name of Jesus.
- Bless his/her home with joy and happiness.
- Give our pastor's spouse a heart to see and meet the needs of our pastor.
- Bless our pastor's children to serve You. (*Pray for adult children as well as young ones. If he/she has no children, pray for him/her to have them.*)
- Father, give our pastor a deserving spouse to help him/her do Your work effectively.
- Deliver our pastor from temptation from the opposite sex or any form of immorality.
- Bless our pastor with perfect health.

- Father, give our pastor strength all the days of his/her life.
- Let our pastor have a real walk with You to the end.
- Deliver our pastor from every form of covetousness.
- Help our pastor to be strong and stand alone, if it ever comes to that.
- Bless our pastor to be an original, not a copy.
- Help our pastor to look unto You alone when it comes to making certain choices.
- Bless our pastor to make You number one in his/her life.
- Bless our pastor financially.
- Supply our Pastor's needs, in Jesus' name.
- Bless our pastor with love for his/her flock.

Chapter 39

BLESSINGS ON YOUR CHURCH MEMBERS

Romans 8:16 says,

> The Spirit itself beareth witness with our
> spirit, that we are the children of God.

Hebrews 8:10 says,

> For this is the covenant that I will make
> with the house of Israel after those days,
> saith the Lord; I will put my laws into their
> mind, and write them in their hearts: and
> I will be to them a God, and they shall be
> to me a people.

1 Peter 2:9–10 says,

> But ye are a chosen generation, a royal priesthood, an holy nation, a peculiar people; that ye should shew forth the praises of Him who hath called you out of darkness into His marvelous light. Which in time past were not a people, but are now the people of God: which had not obtained mercy, but now have obtained mercy.

Prayer:

> ➤ Lord, bless us enter into a permanent relationship with You.
> ➤ Bless us with a mind of accountability for our time, our money, and our lives.
> ➤ Bless us with the strength to choose the mind of Christ.
> ➤ Bless us with the ability to love one another.
> ➤ Bless us with the tenacity to stand alone when making the right choices.
> ➤ Bless us with the boldness to face a corrupt world with the truth of God.

Chapter 40

BLESSINGS ON CHRISTIANS AND THE CHURCH OF THE LORD JESUS CHRIST

Prayer:

- ➤ Lord, bless Your church, the universal church of the Lord Jesus Christ.
- ➤ Lord, let Your church know You; reveal Yourself to the church.
- ➤ Let the people live for You, not for themselves.
- ➤ Bless Your church financially.
- ➤ Bless Christians with substance to move Your work forward.
- ➤ Bless Christians with honest hearts.
- ➤ Bless Christians with the desire to pray.
- ➤ Help Christians to seek Your face daily.

Chapter 41

BLESSINGS ON YOUR PETS

Prayer:

- ➢ Father, bless my pets.
- ➢ Bless my pet with long life.
- ➢ Bless my pet with perfect health.
- ➢ Let my pet be a blessing to my family and me.
- ➢ May God bless my pet with a good caretaker in case it outlives me.

Chapter 42

BLESSINGS ON YOUR FOOD

Prayer:

> ➤ Father, bless my food and let it be a blessing to my body, in Jesus' name.
> ➤ Let the food I eat nourish my body, in Jesus' name.

Chapter 43

BLESSINGS ON YOUR CITY OR VILLAGE

April 15th, 2013, saw a horrendous event in Boston. While the Boston Marathon was in session, bombs started exploding. This was an act born of the evil and cruelty of two brothers. Three people were killed and 264 were injured.

The FBI released photographs and surveillance video of the two suspects, who were eventually identified as Chechen brothers Dzhokhar and Tamerlan Tsarnaev. Next, the brothers killed an MIT police offer, carjacked an SUV, and engaged the police in gunfire battle. Tamerlan died in that gunfight. His brother escaped and hid in a boat in someone's backyard until he was arrested.

If people would take it upon themselves to bless their cities and commit them into the hands of the Almighty God, our cities and villages would be protected. A lot of hurt and heartache would be halted. Historically, many cities are attacked occasionally, but such events are becoming rampant all over the world. Christians are the preservers of the earth; we have to start proving it.

Prayer:

> - Father, bless my city, (*say name of city here*).
> - Bless our city with peace.
> - Protect our city from terrorism.
> - Protect our city from every form of disaster.
> - Build fire walls around our city, in Jesus' name.
> - Bless our city with peaceful and loving people.
> - Bless the people who live in our city with a heart to love our city.
> - Bless the police in our city to have eyes that never misses anything.
> - Protect our city from every form of violence.
> - Protect our city from the violence of bombs and firearms.
> - Father, let Your eyes be upon our city, in Jesus' name.

Chapter 44

BLESSINGS ON YOUR COUNTRY

Prayer:

- ➤ Father, today I bless America (*or substitute with your own nation*).
- ➤ Lord, bless us with good godly leaders, men and women who fear the Lord, so they can make godly decisions.
- ➤ Lord, bless our leaders to lead this country to the next level.
- ➤ Let this country produce great men, and women with great inventions to affect the world.
- ➤ Help us to serve You and serve You well.
- ➤ Fill our hearts with the fear of God.
- ➤ Help this nation to produce honest men.

- Father, transform our deteriorating morals.
- Lord, protect our schools.
- Deliver us from bloodshed in our schools.
- Father, send patrolling angels to protect our schools.
- Father, deliver us from bloodthirsty men.
- Father, help this nation to overcome gun violence, in Jesus' name.
- Let our young ones hear the word of God and implement it.
- Father, help us pay our national debts.
- Let there be love and togetherness in this nation.
- Deliver this nation from segregation and division.
- Bless this nation with good teachers.
- Deliver this nation from every power oppressing us, in Jesus' name.
- Bless us with good and honest law enforcement agents, in Jesus' name.
- Bless our soldiers, and protect them on the field, in Jesus' name.
- Bless this nation with good businesses and new inventions.

➤ Father, change the thinking of our people. Give them a heart for the nation and deliver us from greed. Help the business men and women establish their business here, and not send their businesses to other nations.

Chapter 45

BLESSINGS ON LEADERS OF YOUR NATION

These blessings are for presidents, prime ministers, heads of state, kings, and queens. Even if he or she is not godly, pray for him/her. God will do His part.

Many people make the mistake of spewing evil and talking evil about their leaders. This is wrong.

1 Timothy 2:1–3 says,

> I exhort therefore, that, first of all, supplications, prayers, intercessions, and giving of thanks, be made for all men; For kings, and for all that are in authority; that we may lead a quiet and peaceable life in

all godliness and honesty. For this is good and acceptable in the sight of God our Saviour.

The Bible admonishes us to simply pray for our leaders; therefore, let us do the right thing and leave the judging to the real Judge. He will bring every hidden thing to light at His appearing.

If your leader is a male, address him as such, and if she is a female, address her accordingly.

Prayer:

- Father, bless our president (*or prime minister, king, queen, etc.*).
- Bless his family, his wife, and his children.
- Father, bless him with a revelation to see You.
- Give him wisdom to make the right decisions, that will bless the nation.
- Father, give him godly counselors.
- Father, bless him with godly cabinet members.
- Bless him with good people around him who will not flatter him, but tell him the truth.

> Father, protect his wife and his children.
> Father, bless our president with an honest heart and accountability.
> Father, protect his going out and his coming in, in Jesus' name.

Chapter 46

BLESSINGS OF LAW ENFORCEMENT AGENTS

Prayer for the Police:

- ➢ Father, bless our policemen.
- ➢ Bless them and their entire families.
- ➢ Father, protect them, their going out and their coming in.
- ➢ Father, let there be angelic protection for their lives.
- ➢ Father, give them peace of mind to do their jobs very well.
- ➢ Give them peaceful homes.
- ➢ Give them a heart of love for the country they are serving in.

➢ Give them patience for the people they encounter on a daily basis.

Prayer for Soldiers, Marines, Navy, Military:

➢ Father, bless our soldiers.
➢ Bless our military personnel in foreign lands.
➢ Father, protect them and bring them home safely.
➢ Protect their wives and children.
➢ Protect their husbands and children.
➢ Let the angels of God protect them in their stations.
➢ Father, protect the marines on the seas and at home.
➢ Give them a heart to serve their nation very well.
➢ Father, protect their homes whiles they are on the field, in Jesus' name.

Chapter 47

BLESSINGS ON YOUR CONTINENT

Why is it necessary for God to bless a continent? The first reason is so that, there will be no exodus of every nation on the continent to the one nation that is blessed. The second reason is that there will be no influx of over population from neighboring nations into one country, the country that is blessed on the continent.

It helps when people hear the gospel in their own language. Paul took the gospel to Europe; others took it to Africa and Asia. Now almost everyone has had the chance to hear the gospel.

Acts 16: 9–10 says,

> And a vision appeared to Paul in the night; There stood a man of Macedonia, and prayed him, saying, Come over into Macedonia, and help us. And after he had seen the vision, immediately we endeavoured to go into Macedonia, assuredly gathering that the Lord had called us for to preach the gospel unto them.

Once the gospel hits a nation, it encourages transformation in its people. We must begin to bless our nations because the moment we do, the effects go into motion, and the outcome will be positive. Jesus told us to bless, and curse not.

Our great commission is to go into the world and preach the gospel to every creature.

Mark 16:15 says,

> And he said unto them, Go ye into all the world, and preach the gospel to every creature.

It is our responsibility to do so, but if the land is cursed and there are idols and evil living in the land, it is very difficult for us to have a desire to go.

Once we bless our continent, there will be a ripple effect. The nations and its people will be blessed.

Prayer:

- ➤ Father, I commit (*say name of continent here*) into Your hands. Let Your hand be upon (*say name of continent here*) very strongly.
- ➤ Lord, bless and deliver (*say name of continent here*) from all forms of ammunition.
- ➤ Let all the nations on this continent be blessed.
- ➤ Let the gospel have its course in all the nations of this continent.

- ➤ Bless the people of this Continent to know You and fear You.
- ➤ Let the lands of this continent be blessed.
- ➤ Let the people come to know the true saving knowledge of Jesus Christ.
- ➤ Let the leaders come to know You.
- ➤ Remove satanic leaders from this continent.
- ➤ Touch the hearts of the leaders so they will fear You, in Jesus' name.

Printed in the United States
By Bookmasters